THE UNDERWATER CRIME SCENE

THE UNDERWATER CRIME SCENE

Underwater Crime Investigative Techniques

By

RONALD F. BECKER, J.D.

Department of Criminal Justice
Southwest Texas State University
San Marcos, Texas

CHARLES C THOMAS • PUBLISHER
Springfield • Illinois • U.S.A.

Published and Distributed Throughout the World by

CHARLES C THOMAS • PUBLISHER
2600 South First Street
Springfield, Illinois 62794-9265

© *1995 by* CHARLES C THOMAS • PUBLISHER

ISBN 0-398-05979-9 (cloth)

ISBN 0-398-05980-2 (paper)

Library of Congress Catalog Card Number: 94-48036

Printed in the United States of America
SC-R-3

Library of Congress Cataloging-in-Publication Data

Becker, Ronald F.
    The underwater crime scene : underwater crime investigative
techniques / by Ronald F. Becker.
        p.   cm.
    Includes bibliographical references and index.
    ISBN 0-398-05979-9 (cloth). — ISBN 0-398-05980-2 (paper)
    1. Underwater crime investigation.   2. Police divers.
3. Underwater archaeology—Methodology.   I. Title.
HV8080.D54B43   1995
363.2'5—dc20   94-48036
                                                                  CIP

To
My father Glenn C. Becker, 1918–1994, and
my son Gavin Dixon Becker, born October 8, 1994

FOREWORD

As a police administrator charged with the responsibility of investigating and solving criminal offenses, I am constantly in search of better methods for collecting, processing, and preserving evidence for successful criminal prosecution.

In a city that is literally surrounded by lakes and rivers, and ever increasing development in these areas, I am particularly interested in the recovery of evidence from these waters. Over the last twenty years, there has been very little change in the way underwater recovery of evidence has taken place. The traditional practice of dive teams has been to race to find what is being searched for and quickly recover it without regard for any trace evidence value or preserving the area where it was discovered.

In their zeal to succeed in locating what was being searched for and hopefully catch a criminal or corroborate a statement from a suspect, there has been little emphasis placed on a methodical and thorough examination of the underwater scene or the evidence recovered. The assumption has been that no forensic or trace evidence remains on an item after it is submerged in water, therefore, no need to preserve or process the item as though there were. This book does an excellent job of challenging those assumptions and clearly points out that these assumptions are erroneous.

In recent years, there has been great advancement in the processing, and collection and preserving of evidence discovered on land. This book points out that we now have the technical ability to replicate what we use in our land-based investigations and transfer them to the underwater crime scene. As every criminal investigator and evidence collection expert knows, successfully recovering evidence requires very delicate and precise handling of the crime scene to ensure that the evidence is properly preserved for later examination.

This book explains many techniques and methods to be employed by the underwater evidence search team to enable them to accurately preserve and recover many types of evidence from underwater. Mr. Becker did an exceptional job of combining the techniques used by field and marine archaeologists, criminalists, and forensic scientists to what may emerge as a new field of study. Mr. Becker has presented this material in such a way that this book is a very practical and useful guide that should be employed by every law enforcement agency, fire rescue dive team, and any other investigator who becomes involved in the recovery of evidence from underwater.

Police administrators have an obligation and should have the desire to provide the most up-to-date material for their criminal investigators and this book by Ron Becker certainly meets that criteria.

BRUCE MILLS
Deputy Chief
Austin Police Department
Austin, Texas

PREFACE

All of us who watch the Discovery channel on television know earth is the water planet. The United States has water shrouded boundaries on three sides and inland waterways too numerous to measure. More and more human activity is taking place on America's waterways as we become fully franchised citizens of planet ocean. As our waterborne activities increase, so do the problems associated with enforcing laws on the nation's most popular playgrounds.

Legislatures have passed laws governing citizens' conduct on our diverse waterways and police have met the challenge of enforcing those laws. When crime is committed in, on, or around open water the police have no trouble employing traditional investigative techniques designed to assist in the apprehension of offenders.

Everything taught in investigators' schools and police academies pertaining to crime scene management and processing is seen as inapplicable when dealing with evidence retrieved from underwater. Because of this technical void, most underwater evidence is "salvaged" as opposed to processed. In many instances fire departments have primary responsibility for underwater evidence salvage. Salvage is a process of retrieval that has little concern for the impact of the recovery technique on the item being recovered. Courts, prosecutors, and police have become content with the salvaging of underwater evidence.

Since 1963, a small group of dedicated archaeologists, with a love for the sea and scuba diving, has given birth, nourished, and raised underwater investigation to a science. By utilizing the same type of concepts and techniques as field archaeologists, these individuals have been able to retrieve the remains of ancient ships and their cargoes. Because of painstaking application of patience, scientific method, measurement, photography, sketches, and recovery marine archaeologists have been able to reconstruct vessels and their cargoes from retrieved bits and pieces. They have devised a technology all their own. They have devised a language all their own. They have devised tools and equipment all their own and have discovered a past that the sea has been extremely reluctant to give up.

The work of the marine archaeologists is very similar to that of the police investigator. A trained police investigator can readily see that many of the concerns and objectives of the marine archaeologist are synonymous to the concerns and objectives of the police investigator, the only difference being that of the medium in which each operates.

It is the purpose of this book to bring together the science of the marine archaeologist to the needs of police agencies that have responsibility for providing law enforcement on America's waterways. Much evidence is lost, unrecognized, or mishandled and rendered unusable at the time of trial because of improper handling during the underwater recovery process. Underwater scenes can and should be graphically located, geographically and temporally just as dry land crime scenes are. Chains of custody and demonstrative evidence should be utilized in the presentation of evidence resulting from underwater investigations as they are in any other investigation.

My involvement as a dive specialist with local search and rescue efforts has allowed me to develop an understanding of the restraints operating on police agencies in the training and equipping of search and rescue teams. My practice as a lawyer provided the technical understanding for evidentiary predicates for evidence and the latitude allowed evidence retrieved from waterways. The numerous product defect cases handled by my firm during my practice as a personal injury lawyer gave me an introduction into basic engineering and mechanics. My experience as a police investigator developed an appreciation for the investigative techniques used by police in processing dry land crime scenes. Instructing criminal investigation and introductory forensics courses has contributed to my appreciation of the types of evidence being lost or mishandled in most evidence "salvage" operations. My amateur status and interest in underwater excavations showed me that there is a scientific alternative to what is presently being done. All these experiences have prepared me to write a book dealing with retrieving and processing underwater evidence.

Many experienced investigators will question the practicality of conducting a comprehensive underwater investigation in conditions offering limited visibility or dangerous currents. Admittedly, all the techniques offered in this book cannot be employed in every situation where evidence is attempted to be retrieved from its underwater resting place.

In the future, whenever conditions allow, it will be a mistake to simply salvage evidence when a more scientific approach could have been taken. Investigators in the future will have to qualify the recovery procedures employed and where less was done than could have been, explanations will be expected.

The day of the salvage approach to retrieving evidence ends with this book and a new era of investigative dive specialist is about to dawn. Your interest in this new era of police investigation will allow you to participate in that dawning.

R.F.B.

ACKNOWLEDGMENTS

Diving has been a lifelong passion that has culminated in the writing of this book. All the organized dive schools have contributed to the knowledge imparted to me and necessary for me to safely pursue sport and public utility diving. Discussions with the Austin, Texas Special Response Team were always illuminating and the insights provided by Senior Sergeant Harold Piatt were especially helpful and added a practical flavor to a cerebral endeavor. Deputy Chief Bruce Mills of the Austin Police Department introduced me to Senior Sergeant Piatt and his special response team, which was invaluable in gathering material included in this book. Marty Lee of Boerne, Texas provided the illustrations that have added a living dimension to the text.

CONTENTS

THE UNDERWATER CRIME SCENE

Chapter 1

INTRODUCTION

MAN AND THE SEA

More than 70 percent of the earth's surface is covered with water. Since earliest time humans have been drawn to the earth's waters for trade, transportation, recreation, and food. Greeks, as early as 4500 B.C., were free diving in the Mediterranean. Accounts of Heredities, the Greek historian, describe the efforts of free divers in salvaging sunken treasure (Diole', 1951). Entry into the underwater realm was undoubtedly linked with the transit of goods by vessel. Ocean trade and war gave rise to the need for salvage activities. Free diving was limited in depth and duration. It was inevitable that efforts would be made to use "machines" to allow divers to increase both depth and duration. Aristotle wrote in 330 B.C. of divers using a diving bell made of leather and later of pitch bound wood (Diole', 1951).

Today, divers using compressed air can safely dive unfettered to depths of one hundred feet. In the last thirty years, technology and education have moved diving from the purview of the strong and courageous and placed it in the world of recreation and sport.

UNDERWATER ARCHAEOLOGY AS A SCIENCE

In the world of science, underwater archaeology is in its infancy. The popularizing of wartime diving by the media gave rise to a national curiosity about navy "frogmen," and to a 1960s television program called "Sea Hunt." Interest increased with the Jacque Cousteau television specials and a James Bond film called "Thunderball." People were no longer content watching others dive. Sport diving was born and its popularity has continued to grow. That growth and development has been closely linked to the fledgling science of underwater archaeology.

It was not until 1974 that academe was ready to embrace underwater archaeology. In that year the University of California at San Diego became the first to offer an undergraduate degree in underwater archaeology. Today there are only seven universities in the world offering a graduate curriculum in underwater archaeology (Marx, 1990).

Utilizing excavation techniques similar to those used in land excavations, these new scientists have been able to recover artifacts from sunken cities and reconstruct much of that city's history and culture. They have been able to excavate entire vessels, and from their cargoes, deduce place of origin, trade routes, and personal information about crew and passengers. Contrary to popular belief, many artifacts survive better in water than on land.

Many field archaeologists were of the opinion that marine archaeology would never meet the rigors of the science of archaeology. Critics viewed early underwater archaeological activity as a salvaging or looting of artifacts. The artifacts that were being recovered by these "treasure hunters" were not being properly handled, processed, or preserved and in short order deteriorated and became useless (Taylor, 1965). No information was being gathered in situ. It is the field archaeologist's belief that it is her responsibility to record the location of each artifact or piece of artifact because, as in a criminal investigation, what may have little relevance or significance now, may prove invaluable later. It took time and attention to detail but a slowly evolving science emerged from the watery depths applying the same techniques that field archaeologists applied. The underwater archaeologist is in every sense of the word an underwater investigator. These individuals now have the keys to unlock the richest museum in the world.

LAW ENFORCEMENT AND UNDERWATER EVIDENCE

People flock to recreational waterways in vast numbers. As the number of people using recreational waterways increases so do the number of accidents, drownings, violent crimes, and homicides. Criminals often seek a watery repository for weapons and other evidence of wrongdoing. It has become an integral part of the police function to provide resources that can be deployed to retrieve this evidence. Historically, fire departments have provided these services to the police since they already had firefighters who were trained in search and rescue diving. It was believed that no special skills other than diving were required to provide these services. The handling and processing of underwater evidence was a salvage operation.

The first accounts of a dedicated (specific as to function) police underwater evidence recovery team appeared in Dade County, Florida. The Dade County Underwater Recovery Unit began in 1960 and has had the responsibility for 28 cities, 400 miles of inland canals, over 400 rock quarries and 75 miles of bay front (Robinson, 1969).

As we view existing dedicated dive recovery operations, it is apparent they have evolved and been criticized much the same as early underwater archaeologists. Police recovery of underwater evidence could also be criticized for an absence of scientific rigor, focusing on salvage rather than recovery and reconstruction.

What information is lost in the salvage process? What might be inferred from measurement, sketches, and photographs, if not at the time of discovery, perhaps later? What parts of the story remain untold because of a failure to properly handle and package evidence, thereby preventing forensic examination? What value is salvaged material if it cannot be entered into evidence because of a failure to connect the evidence with the defendant? If a piece of evidence were located on land, no competent investigator would pick it up, hold it over his head and say "I've found it." Contrary to popular belief, forensic evidence is not necessarily lost when it has been immersed in water.

REFERENCES

Diole', P. H. (1954). *4,000 Years Under The Sea.* New York: John Jay Press.

Marx, Robert F. (1990). *The Underwater Dig.* Houston: Gulf Publishing Company.

Robinson, Peg (1969). County Frogmen Always Ready For Anything. *The Christian Science Monitor.* Mar 17.

Taylor, Joan du Platt (1969). *Marine Archaeology,* London: Tavistock.

Chapter 2

LEGAL LIABILITY AND
THE UNDERWATER RECOVERY PROCESS

Police retrieval of underwater evidence is a relatively new proposition. In the aftermath of the Branch Dividian siege in Waco, Texas, a basement area had gathered sufficient water to require the services of a dive recovery team to determine if there were submerged bodies; unfortunately no divers were available. In those departments that have recovery teams, much concern has arisen regarding the cost benefit analysis. Few departments have dedicated dive operations (teams that provide only dive services) separately funded. In many instances, departments have used special team personnel (S.W.A.T.) and funds for their diving needs. Often responsibility for dive activities falls to any officer with dive experience. Administrators who do not dive have limited understanding of the recovery process. The presumption is that a diver is a diver. Sport divers have little preparation for limited/no visibility diving (black water diving) and may be as susceptible to risk in that milieu as are nondivers.

VICARIOUS LIABILITY

A municipality or a police department may be held responsible for the injurious conduct of its police officers if the municipality or department contributed to or condoned the conduct that gave rise to that injury (*Monell v. New York Department of Social Services,* 436 U.S. 658, 1978). This type of responsibility is referred to in the law of torts as vicarious liability, i.e., an employer's responsibility for the conduct of his employee. The conduct required in suits alleging vicarious liability may be as a result of municipal and departmental policies (*Springfield v. Kibbe,* 480 U.S. 808, 1987).

SUPERVISORY LIABILITY

From a lawyer's perspective, suing a police officer is not as financially rewarding as finding a method whereby the department and/or the municipality may be joined as parties, thereby increasing the depth of the pocket from which a verdict may be satisfied. Departmental supervisors are considered to be representatives of the department and the municipality. If a supervisor condones or contributes to conduct of one of his subordinates who caused injury, the municipality and department may now also be held responsible (*Oklahoma City v. Tuttle,* 474 U.S. 808, 1985). This type of responsibility is referred to in the law of torts as supervisory liability.

In discussing issues of vicarious and supervisory liability, the parties usually involved are an injured citizen and an injuring police officer. However, the same conduct on the part of a department that could give rise to an injury to a member of the public, may also give rise to injury to police and more specifically to injuries incurred during underwater dive operations. Municipalities and departments have learned painful and expensive lessons in negligence lawsuits. Departments and municipalities have been found negligent in situations where citizens have been injured as a result of a lack of police training that was the proximate cause of that citizen's injury. Attention must be paid to the cases that have held departments and municipalities liable for failing to provide officers necessary equipment or training to safely fulfill the responsibilities levied upon them by their supervisors and departments (*City of Canton, Ohio v. Harris et al.* 489 U.S. 378, 1988). Departments that require officers to respond to a dangerous situation without the necessary equipment, supervision or training may be responsible for that officer's injuries. In those states without the exclusive remedy of workmen's compensation laws, departments and municipalities may be parties to negligence suits brought by injured officers. In those states with workmen's compensation laws, gross negligence may still allow suits by injured officers.

If a department has determined there is a need for an underwater recovery team, it must consider the inherent risks associated with that decision. In arriving at that decision municipalities and department administrators must commit themselves to providing the necessary tools, supervision, and training. Absent that commitment, the associated risks of underwater recovery are too high.

STANDARD OPERATIONS AND PROCEDURES MANUALS

It is axiomatic in the law enforcement business that if it is not in the Standard Operations and Procedures Manual (S.O.P.), it does not exist. When confronted with a lawsuit, a department's success or failure may often depend on the contents of that manual. When examined from a legal perspective, that manual should be viewed as canonical. The department is often stretched upon a rack of its own manufacture when the department's Standard Operations and Procedures manual is exposed to the light of day. Every aspect of the law enforcement function should be described in that manual in current and specific detail. There is no avoiding S.O.P. manuals. If a department does not have one, you lose. If it is not current, same result. If it is not complete, liability may result. If the operations manual does not reflect that all personnel understand and agree to abide by the contents, liability may attach. When kept, maintained, and applied correctly, the lives of citizens are protected. When kept, maintained, and applied correctly, the lives of police officers are protected. When kept, maintained, and applied correctly, departments and municipalities will prevail in lawsuits based on vicarious liability and negligence.

S.O.P. MANUALS AND UNDERWATER RECOVERY

All departments have an operations manual. The quality of that manual will depend upon the commitment of the municipality and department in providing information, rules, guidelines and training to all personnel. The department must have a lawyer familiar with criminal law, constitutional law, civil rights law, and tort law as a constant resource, overseer, and collaborator in the maintenance of the operations manual.

That manual as it pertains to the underwater recovery team must address the following:

1. Selection Criteria

All employment criteria must be nondiscriminatory, merit-based, and open to all officers who meet that criteria. Any physical, experiential, or mental requirements must be job-related. The burden of proving that relationship rests upon departmental policy makers. All criteria must be free of gender, race, or age bias.

Historically, special teams have been the purview of young male officers; that should not be viewed as a precedent. There is little in the world of the underwater investigator that is dependent on strength. Patience, imagination, and thought are the tools of the underwater recovery specialist. Women have certain definite physiological advantages for underwater work: less air consumption, and greater resistance to cold. Virtually everything handled in the water becomes buoyant or can be made so, therefore abrogating the need for applications of strength. An appropriate adage for underwater work might be "work smart, not strong."

2. Certification

Basic swimming skills will be necessary to obtain dive certification. Advanced certification in search and rescue demands more from a diver. As a dive master, required competency in the water is again increased. By requiring each team member to obtain dive master certification from an accredited dive organization, the department will have acquired the necessary swimming skills for team performance. All divers should have advanced open water certification, search and rescue certification, dive master certification, experience in underwater photography, and black water training. It would increase the versatility of the team if one diver was rated as an instructor with black water and salvage certification. Having a team member with an instructor's rating will allow inservice training and periodic checkout dives to be conducted with little cost to the agency.

3. Histories of Claustrophobia

Limited visibility may adversely affect those individuals uncomfortable in closed places. There will be situations where divers may be required to enter sunken vessels or vehicles, both such environments may pose problems for the claustrophobic.

4. Type "A" Personalities

Type "A" personalities gravitate to special mission teams. Action-oriented persons are an advantage in those situations where special tactics may need to be employed. Underwater, strategy is more important than tactics, and patience is an absolute necessity. Type "A" personalities may be an asset to tactical operations, but they are a liability to underwater operations.

5. Basic Math and Measurement Skills

Much of what we discuss in subsequent chapters will involve applied math in interpreting dive tables, underwater direction finding, land and underwater use of measuring devices.

6. Histories of Vertigo

Looking down from the surface after entering water with unrestricted visibility gives one the sensation of height. Individuals fearing heights may be placed in an untenable position when entering deep clear water.

7. Medical Histories of Heart Disease

Although physical exertion underwater is generally unnecessary, stress is an integral part of the underwater evidence recovery process. Although stress is a part of all police work, it can be seriously magnified when encumbered by limited visible support personnel. Individuals with histories of coronary problems may be placed in an inhospitable environment where recourse to medical assistance is distant.

8. Diving During Pregnancy

There is limited empirical data pertaining to the effects of nitrogen absorption and increased atmospheric pressure on the unborn fetus. In the absence of definitive data it is better to be cautious and ban diving during pregnancies.

9. Medical Histories Involving Inner Ear Problems

Changing atmospheric pressures requires an adjustment of pressure within the ear. Often this adjustment does not occur spontaneously and requires the diver to assist manually to clear the pressure by holding his nose and gently blowing through his nose, gradually increasing the force with which he is blowing his nose until the ears equalize the pressure. Persons with inner ear problems may have difficulty equalizing that pressure or may aggravate a preexisting injury when attempting to do so.

10. Alcohol or Drug Use

The same restrictions regarding alcohol and drug use that the department has adopted obviously apply to all aspects of police work. The underwater recovery team member may be on call or conscripted during off-duty hours. Any alcohol consumption prior to diving will impair the judgement of the diver, placing the diver and the team at risk. The underwater world is less forgiving of mistakes. Prescribed medications and over-the-counter pharmaceuticals are tested at surface atmospheric pressure. The effects of drugs at depth under pressure, recombining with nitrogen are generally unknown.

11. Physical Requirements

Instead of height to weight ratios which have been applied discriminatorily in the past, it would be more useful to apply a percentage of body fat measurement for physical fitness. Again it is important to stress that any such physical requirements be job-related and the burden is upon the employer to demonstrate that relationship.

12. Testing

Each diver having been tentatively selected for the dive team regardless of certification should perform an in-water test to allow an evaluation of that individual's response to stress in the water. At the time of selection and every six months thereafter all underwater recovery team members should be required to qualify through a refresher of basic diving skills which should include: (1) mask clearing at depth; (2) buddy breathing at depth; (3) mouthpiece removal and reinsertion at depth; (4) mask removal and replacement at depth; (5) emergency ascent with air; (6) emergency ascent without air; (7) removal of buoyancy compensator and air supply and surfacing; (8) removal of buoyancy compensator and air supply and replacing same; (9) boat entries; (10) land entries; (11) drown proofing; (12) 250 meter uninterrupted freestyle swim; (13) 25 meter underwater swim; (14) demonstrate accepted rescue techniques for assisting injured or unconscious divers.

13. Fitness Reports

Semiannual fitness reports should be performed and maintained for each diving member. No diver should be allowed to participate in a recovery operation after a diveless period in excess of 90 days. Checkout dives should be performed and documented for each diver who has been out of the water for 90 days.

The foregoing are examples of minimum policy and procedure considerations that should be included in Standard Operations and Procedures Manuals pertaining to dive recovery operations and teams. Failure to include underwater recovery operations in the Standard Operations and

Procedures Manual can be catastrophic in two ways. Not only can failure to specify expectations and responsibilities result in unnecessary and costly litigation, but officers who know what is expected of them are more likely to be able to meet those expectations. Team leaders will have objective criteria upon which to make selection and disciplinary decisions.

Operating manuals are being viewed by the courts as contracts between citizens, police, police departments, and municipalities; they are documents of accountability. Failure on the part of departments and municipalities to fashion workable standard operations and procedures manuals and to meet the terms of these "contracts" may result in suit, injury, or death.

REFERENCES

St. Louis v. Praprotnik, 485 U.S. 112 (1988).
Los Angeles v. Heller, 475 U.S. 796 (1986).
Polk County v. Dodson, 454 U.S. 312 (1981).
Fiacco v. Rensselaer, 783 F.2nd. 319 (CA2 1986).
Patzner v. Burkett, 779 F.2nd. 1363 (CA8 1985).
Languirand v. Hayden, 717 F.2nd. 220 (CA5 1983).

TABLE OF CASES

City of Canton, Ohio v. Harris et al., 489 U.S. 378 (1988).
Monell v. New York Department of Social Services, 436 U.S. 658 (1978).
Oklahoma City v. Tuttle, 474 U.S. 808 (1985).
Springfield v. Kibbe, 480 U.S. 257 (1987).

Chapter 3

BEGINNING THE INVESTIGATION

GATHERING INFORMATION

The focus in land investigations is on witnesses. Witnesses are as important to the underwater recovery team as they are to any investigative effort. When dealing with drownings or abandoned evidence, where witnesses are available, the dive team should not rely on investigators to gather information pertaining to the "last point seen." The dive team has responsibility to establish independently the last seen point. A thorough examination of possible witnesses by a member of the dive team may provide "last point seen" data overlooked or misinterpreted by the investigating officers. That information may reduce the time and effort expended in the search of the applicable areas.

In drownings, the victim is often found on the bottom within a radius from the last seen point which is equal to the depth of the water. For example, if the victim were drowned in 30 feet of water, the body may be found on the bottom within a 30 foot radius from the point on the bottom directly below the "last seen point" topside. In establishing the "last seen point" it is often helpful to place a diver or a boat in the water and allow the witness to direct the diver to the "last seen point." All interviews should be conducted at the scene approximating the location of the witness at the time of the sighting. The effectiveness of developing a "last seen point," and the futility of not using one, was demonstrated when a boat was sunk in a lake surrounded by a residential community. The first divers on the scene inquired of individuals at the scene the general area in which the boat sank, then cleared the area of all civilians. They searched for five days without success. A second team was later dispatched and began canvassing the houses overlooking the area in question. Utilizing a boat placed on the lake as a reference point various witnesses placed the point at some distance from that first determined to be the "last seen point." The sunken boat was discovered shortly after the new search began. The difference in the approaches of the two dive teams was

13

that the first divers were relying on conjecture fueled by haste, rather than using a search strategy beginning with interviews based on a floating reference point. Although the second team spent a day in seeking and interviewing witnesses, their total on site time was two days culminating in a successful operation as opposed to the five fruitless days spent by the first team.

All information gathered from witnesses or other investigators is geared to provide information that will assist in the recovery of physical evidence. Witnesses differ in perspective and investigators may color that information through their own perspectives. Any information provided by investigators pertaining to the search area should be corroborated if possible. Obviously it will take additional time to reinterview those witnesses, but time spent pinpointing the search area is time well spent. Information gathered by the dive team's intelligence officer should be documented and provided to the officers in charge of the investigation. Although the recovery of drowning victims gets the most media exposure, underwater recovery teams spend most of their time in the water seeking evidence usually in the form of a weapon, stolen property, or abandoned drugs.

As waterway recreation and transportation expands, so will crimes committed on those waterways. Police divers provide a large range of recovery services including but not limited to:

boat arsons
suicides
homicides
drownings
abandoned contraband
abandoned weapons
abandoned vehicles
vehicle entombment
vessel and aircraft crashes and contraband attached to keels.

THE UNDERWATER CRIME SCENE

The first step in any underwater investigation is to locate the underwater crime scene. It is helpful to think of the recovery of underwater evidence as an extension of the overall investigation. By perceiving the recovery operation as an integral part of the overall investigation, it is but one short step to viewing the underwater operation as the processing of a crime scene. If the offense suspected is such that it would precipitate a crime scene analysis, then the underwater counterpart of that investigation should be conducted as meticulously.

As in any investigation, a search cannot begin until a reasonable search area has been delineated and all information that might reduce the size of the search area is gathered and considered. Much underwater time and frustration can be avoided by not entering the water too soon.

In most instances of police diving the life of the victim is not in question. Bad weather and surface conditions should be considered before anyone is ordered into the water. Barring a hurricane, the bottom conditions tomorrow will be virtually the same as today. Postponing the dive until better diving conditions are available should be a constant consideration in the mind of the team leader. There is no evidence so important that it warrants risking the life of a diver.

Divers are often requested to recover an item of evidence that is partially visible or has already been located. Where the resting place of the item sought can be ascertained from the surface, it is not necessary to initiate search procedures. In those instances where it is incumbent upon the recovery team to conduct the search the following general procedures should be employed.

SEARCH BRIEFING

Once the area of the search has been described a search briefing should be conducted describing the methods to employ and the roles for each participant. Often dive teams are eager to get into the water and lack of planning results in an initial search that proves fruitless, resulting in a duplication of time and effort.

An integral part of the briefing is documenting the dive. The following information should be obtained and documented for inclusion in the dive report:

a. witnesses interviewed: names, addresses and telephone numbers
b. dive team members
c. date
d. time
e. location
f. persons present
g. purpose of search

  h. time arrived
  i. time search begun
  j. methods of searches conducted
  k. weather conditions
  l. water conditions: temperature, depth, tide, current
  m. bottom conditions
  n. equipment availability: vessels, tow trucks, barges
  o. time, date, and reason for terminating search.

BOTTOM STRUCTURE

Determining bottom structure will help in selecting search methods and equipment. Many freshwater sites have silt and mud bottoms. Limited visibility can be further hampered by stirring up sediment. It is apparent that in searches involving mud and silt bottoms that buoyancy control will be important. Depth will have to be maintained above the bottom at a distance that will allow visual examination of the bottom without stirring up mud. When dealing with bottoms of this nature searches should be conducted in layers, beginning at the farthest reaches of visibility and descending closer to the bottom in stages. Inland lake bottoms may be covered with decayed vegetation on top of mud or silt, additionally hampering a search effort. Often the only sign of evidence may be the depression or disturbance caused by the item as it settled to the bottom.

Current

Current is important for two reasons. First, it may require that mechanical assistance be provided to the diver to maintain a position in the current and to prevent being moved by the current. Second, police not familiar with underwater operations may exaggerate the effect of the current when locating the search area. In river searches where fast currents are evident, it may be necessary to affix a line across the river securely anchored on both sides. Once anchored, another line can be tied into the base line perpendicularly to allow the search divers a hand hold on to which an underwater sled can be attached. Underwater sleds are available commercially, but limited mechanical and wood working skills are all that are required in making one.

Conventional wisdom suggests that in fast currents, items dropped will flow with the current and may be great distances downriver from the

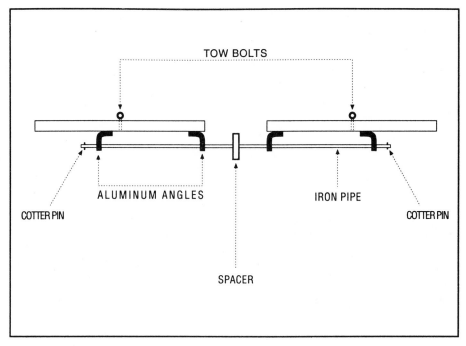

Figure 1. Underwater sled construction: side view.

entry sight. Despite this, it will prove expedient in the long run to begin all searches at the point of entry. Items, including bodies, often are not affected by the current and lie below the point of entry.

Surf, Waves and Tide

Turbulent surface activity in shallow water may affect items reposing on the bottom. Again the effect of surf and waves may not be as great as expected and search operations should begin at the point of entry. Obviously, tides and crashing surf may move material shoreward or out to sea, but presumptions made as to the degree of movement may be erroneous.

Knowing the tide characteristics of a potential dive sight can affect the search in a number of ways that do not directly act on submerged evidence. When interviewing witnesses about the "last point seen," tide must be taken into consideration because it can affect the witnesses' distance perception. If possible, such witnesses should be interviewed at the scene at approximately the same tidal flow as the incident in question. In areas of significant tidal flux, awaiting low tide may allow a search of the area without the necessity of entering the water.

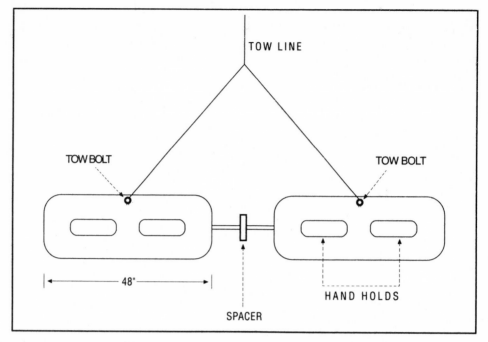

Figure 2. Underwater sled construction: top view.

Most waves are generated by winds beginning their journey far out at sea. The size of a wave depends on the speed of the wind, the length of time a gust of wind blows, and the distance the wind traverses over the water (Bondy, 1993:64). A chart has been developed, called the Beaufort Wind Scale, to show the relationship between wind velocity and wave height. There are two parts to a wave: the crest and the trough. The larger the difference between the wave crest and trough, the larger the wave. The distance between wave crests is called the wavelength.

The way a wave looks is determined by wind, water depth, and bottom structure. As waves approach the shore through increasingly shallow water, friction with the bottom begins to drag on the wave. The distance between waves decreases, causing the wave's energy to make its height increase. When a wave reaches an area where the water depth is about one and one-third times the height of the wave, it will collapse forward upon itself creating a "wave break" (Bondy, 1993:65).

The first thing divers need to understand about entering the sea through waves is timing. Waves pulse onto a beach in a certain rhythm, called a set. A set is created when two or more waves created from different forces meet at sea. Each of these waves is on a different wavelength.

Occasionally wavelengths coincide creating a wave larger than the others, this is called a set "peak." Wavelengths will coincide for a few moments before they conflict. Eventually one wave's crest will occur at the same time as the other's trough. This causes a canceling effect called a "lull." The cycle of waves and lulls continues until the waves strike the beach.

There are usually five to nine waves in a set (Bondy, 1993:65). It is advisable to time the number of waves between the larger set "peaks" to determine the set rhythm before initiating beach recovery operations. Reading sets will allow the recovery team to enter the water as the weakest waves reach the beach, then swim into or beyond the surf zone.

WEATHER

Some dive operations must take place in the most severe weather conditions. Those involving rescue efforts often occur in dangerous weather conditions. Most evidence recovery operations do not need to be undertaken in severe weather. Police may feel an obligation to prove to their peers or the public that, like the postman, weather is to be ignored. If search or recovery operations are being conducted with the assistance of a boat, weather may be of greater concern to the boat crew than the dive team. Nonetheless, an extensive recovery operation should not be begun without some consideration of the weather. Relying on television broadcasts or newspaper weather reports may not provide the most current weather information available. There are three VHF frequencies used by the National Oceanic and Atmospheric Administration for its NOAA Weather Radio broadcasts. The National Weather Service, which is part of NOAA, broadcasts continuous forecasts and reports of current weather on these frequencies. In and around coastal areas, weather radios also broadcast marine forecasts and advisories. The ultimate in weather radios are those that turn on automatically when the Weather Service broadcasts a special signal.

Sailors have always been interested in the weather. Folk predictions of weather no longer occupy an important place in our daily activities. Not being weather dependent in terms of our employment, most of us rely on weather broadcasts. That reliance is most important in conducting underwater search and recovery operations.

PERIMETER MARKING

The preliminary briefing should be followed by dispatching divers to mark the perimeter of the area to be searched with buoys and, if necessary, to place a dive flag visible to any vessels that may be using the area. A rectangle is generally used to describe the perimeter with each corner marked with buoys that are visible not only to team participants but also by any vessel traffic. The size of these buoys should be large enough not to be ignored. Many boundary markers are fifty-five gallon drums painted red with a white stripe designating a dive operation. Rings can be welded to the drums through which rope can be tied. The end of the rope should be equipped with a fitting that will allow various types of anchoring devices to be attached (grappling hook, anchor, cement blocks) accommodating various bottom structures, water and weather conditions. Commercial buoys are available for those departments with budgets allowing such purchases.

Once the perimeter has been marked, it should be located geographically (by transit, compass, or range finder) and sketched or plotted on a site map. If a site map is drawn or available, plastic overlays allow plotting the search area onto the plat without permanently marking the map itself. If the search area must be expanded, the overlay can be replaced. Each overlay should be kept as a permanent part of the dive record so that testimony regarding the search can be supported by the plastic overlays. The search area can be expanded by moving two corners of the rectangles designating the original search area, thereby creating the new area to be searched. Once the search area perimeter has been marked the recovery process can begin.

REFERENCE

Bondy, C. 1993. Waves: A sign of things to come. *Dive Trainer,* March 1993.

Chapter 4

THE UNDERWATER RECOVERY TEAM

BLACK WATER DIVING

Many nondivers and sport divers believe that the police diver's job is fun, much like the film footage seen on television and in the movies. Film footage is shot in water with visibility in excess of 100 feet. In reality, police diving often is done in water of visibility of less than 3 feet. When that visibility drops to less than six inches a whole new set of variables is thrust upon that diver.

Black water diving does not depend on the sense of sight. In many instances a reliance on sight when visibility is limited is detrimental if not fatal. In a no gravity environment, without sight, how does one determine "up"? Without sight, how does a diver determine his depth? Without sight, how does a diver tell in which cardinal direction he is travelling? Without sight, how does a diver tell how much air is left in his tank? Without sight, how does a diver tell how long he has been submerged? None of these questions need be addressed by the diver who can rely upon his sight. Depth gauges, air gauges, compasses, and watches have been the tools divers have historically relied upon to provide input about their support systems and environment. The "black water" diver depends on his teammates to convey the necessary information to him. More equipment is being developed as you read this to address the specific needs for the technical diving often required of underwater recovery divers. But much of the technique used has been a process of trial and error, injury and death.

Touch is the sense upon which the low visibility diver must depend. With all other senses rendered dysfunctional, the focus of sensory input is upon the hands. All data upon which the diver is normally dependent must reach him through his tactile senses. In underwater recovery operations that data is often relayed by team members through tactile sensed communications. It is imperative that each team member trusts explicitly those who comprise the team. The confidence that underwater recovery team divers have in each other is literally based on "blind faith."

BUILDING THE TEAM

A dive team is a dynamic creature that must be nourished and cultivated. Nothing about diving or dive operations remains the same. An integral part of a dive operation is the bringing together of persons best suited for the task. Suitability, in this instance, cannot be predicated upon gender, rank, or seniority. If something or someone becomes an obstacle to the overall productivity of the team and its function, there must be a built-in mechanism to replace that component. No person or component is more important than the organization.

COORDINATING BOARD

Although not a part of the operational end of the dive recovery team, a dive team coordinating board is the political action group for the team. The coordinating board should include in its membership a doctor, lawyer, senior dive team officer, or dive team leader. This organization handles the daily and long-range administrative needs of the department dive recovery team which may include:

    spokespeople to agency administrators
    politicians
    media and external funding agencies
    policy makers
    budget oversight
    equipment selection and update
    discipline
    team selection, recruitment, and termination
    record keeping entity for dive recovery operations.

TEAM MEMBERS

The role of team members should be explicitly understood. Recovery team members may exchange roles or perform more than one, but each role should be specifically described and areas of responsibility clearly defined. Each team should include:

1. A Team Leader

It is his or her responsibility to organize and supervise the entire operation. It is the team leader's responsibility to act as liaison with any other departments, agencies, or investigators. The team leader should not participate in the "in-water" operation. It is imperative that the team leader be available to make decisions pertaining to the overall operation. In the water is not the best place from which to command a perspective for those decisions.

If a problem arises in the water which threatens divers, there must be someone available who knows the respective strengths and weaknesses of all the team members. There must be someone who is capable of bringing to bear all necessary logistics and manpower.

The morale and discipline of the team is a reflection of the team leader's philosophy. By setting and enforcing hiring, qualification, and training standards the status of his or her team is enhanced or denigrated proportionately. The safety of the team in the water may depend upon the equipment the team leader selects and how that equipment is maintained and updated. Courtroom success will be dependent to a large degree on the documentation and record keeping maintained by the team leader, which should include:

training files
medical records
offense reports
incident reports
complaints
disciplinary actions
commendations
dive logs and debriefings
decompression records
dive narratives
recovery documentation
evidence logs.

2. A Dive Master.

It is this team member who is responsible for the underwater operation. That responsibility begins long before the team is dispatched to a dive site. It is the dive master's responsibility to select team members for the operation in question and gather all equipment and logistical support necessary. He is responsible for the team briefing wherein entry sites, measurement, and evidence processing requirements are discussed. The dive master is responsible for the predive briefing wherein in water depths, temperatures, currents, and tides are discussed. Anticipated dive depths should be considered and dive profiles drawn. Once the search area has been delineated the dive master should outline the search methods to be employed. Each dive should be recorded as to time, depth, and personnel. Dive logs tracking depth, time, and nitrogen absorption should be kept for each dive and each diver. It is the dive master who determines who goes in the water, when they go in the water, and when they come back out. It is the dive master who debriefs each diver after each dive and conducts a team debriefing at the end of each day's diving as well as upon completion of the dive operation. These debriefings should assist in the completion of a narrative describing the operation, its successes and failures.

3. Intelligence Officer

Each team should have at least one officer who is responsible for gathering all intelligence pertaining to the intended dive site and evidence to be recovered.

4. Photographer

Each team should have a photographer assigned in those instances where water visibility allows photographic recording of the recovery procedure. A photographic record of the dive site and approaches to that location may prove helpful to investigators.

5. Recovery Specialists

All team members should be specialists in the location, measurement, identification, tagging, handling, and processing of underwater evidence. Subsequent chapters will describe the types of forensic evidence that are not eradicated by water and the prospective sites of such potential evidence. Methods of underwater processing, recovery, measurement, and preservation of evidence will also be discussed.

6. Training Coordinator

One member of the team should be identified as having training responsibilities. That does not necessarily imply that the training coordinator be expected to conduct all training. This team member is responsible for organizing all activities, consistent with inservice and initial training requirements as set forth in the standard operations and procedures manual. An integral part of training is document maintenance. Accurate records should be maintained detailing dates, time, and content of all training provided. In addition to training activities, conducting annual or semiannual qualification exercises is the responsibility of the training coordinator. It would prove helpful if this team member had in addition to an instructor's rating "black water diving" and salvage certification and experience.

This team member is responsible for providing all initial training to new team members.

7. Archivist

Any on-site measurements, sketches, records or reports should be kept by someone who appreciates the need for accuracy and legibility. Few police officers enjoy paperwork; however, concise records allow for more efficient report writing and testimony. It is of little value to be an excellent investigator if reports are embarrassingly illegible and in-court testimony is ponderous or convoluted. A policeman's career is often dependent on communication skills, including ability and inclination to keep accurate and legible records as well as the skills to testify about those records.

8. Equipment Specialist

The equipment specialist should routinely check all equipment and every six months perform required maintenance on all dive equipment. Periodic maintenance checks must be documented for each piece of diving equipment used by all dive team members. Any equipment issued by the department should be kept under lock and key for use in police operations only. All equipment should be checked prior to issue and again upon return. It is important that these equipment checks are not conducted to place blame in the event of damage but rather in the interests of the divers in having safe and operational equipment available. Divers should be discouraged from using personal equipment. It should be understood by all team members that any equipment used on a dive other than departmental equipment is not authorized and any such use absolves the department of liability for injury or death resulting from such use.

Most departments do not have the manpower or funds to provide all of the specialists listed above. It is understood that team divers may wear more than one hat. Every operation will not require the use of all team members. As in any crime scene it will be the responsibility of the investigating officers to determine the extent of crime scene processing. The time spent and quality of the evidence recovery operation should be commensurate with the offense in question and the quality of the investigation overall.

TRAINING

There have developed a number of training schools or programs that provide entry level diving skills for the sport diver. Many dive team applicants will have basic skills certification and some advanced training. To assure consistency in operational activities it is imperative to introduce each new diver to "the way the team does things." A reintroduction to basic skills will remedy any deficits in the new diver's initial training. New diver training should include:

1. orientation sessions pertaining to safety policies
2. orientation session as to most common waters dived, including current, tide, and prevalent wind information pertinent to each area in which the dive team may be called on to perform
3. review of the physics of diving gases, dive tables, and dive computers
4. review management of decompression sickness
5. review decompression dives, uses and abuses
6. review recompression protocol
7. review diver rescue procedures
8. review basic first aid/advanced first aid
9. review search procedures
10. review underwater communication including low visibility tug and squeeze signals
11. perform stress tests both in high visibility and simulated zero visibility conditions
12. review navigation by compass and compass searches
13. underwater police photography
14. review session covering salvage operations, including line and light and medium lift techniques
15. review of methods of tending divers above and below the surface, including line handling and signals

16. instruction in the use of archaeological measurement techniques above and below the water
17. review of search procedures
18. instruction in the use of underwater archaeological techniques used in the recovery of evidence and bodies
19. wreck penetration
20. review moving water operations
21. review frozen water operations
22. night diving
23. deep diving
24. altitude diving
25. beach deployment
26. helicopter deployment
27. deployment by rappelling.

Undoubtedly a lengthy list, but it should be borne in mind that the majority of the skills listed should already be possessed by the trainee and the sessions suggested are an opportunity for the training officer to evaluate, not teach those skills. It is the training officer's responsibility to see how well these skills have been learned and to supplement or disqualify where necessary. It would be impossible to give initial training the attention it deserves in less than 80 hours. No trainee should be allowed to participate in the water, in a team recovery operation, until he has completed the above listed activities.

Upon completion of the suggested training procedure outlined, the trainee should be accepted on a probationary basis. The period of probation should last 90 to 180 days or be terminated upon recommendation of the training officer.

Chapter 5

THE SEARCH

It is not always necessary to launch a search utilizing large numbers of men and expensive equipment. In waters of high visibility, fishermen for centuries have used a simple device to locate underwater schools of fish. This same device, a glass bottom bucket, should be part of every recovery team's equipment. Edmund Scientific of New Jersey makes an inflatable cone with a glass bottom and a viewfinder top designed specifically for clear water use. Getting in the water is not always the most effective use of manpower and time.

BOAT SEARCHES

Identifying the search area may begin with a slow boat ride over the area peering through a glass bottom bucket. Looking through a glass bottomed bucket relegates boat speed to two or three knots. A faster method may be to tow a diver behind the boat using snorkel and fins or a search sled. When towing a diver, it is important to provide him tow rope of sufficient length to avoid prop wash distortion and motor fumes. If the search is to be a prolonged one, utilization of a sled will reduce arm fatigue and the necessity for rapid diver replacement. Sled searches enable boat operators to follow a surface pattern much easier to maintain and control resulting in a more efficient use of time, manpower, and assures a more accurate search has been conducted. When the diver sees what might be the object of the search he can drop off the rope or drop a small fisherman's buoy that unreels line as the weighted end drops to the bottom. These buoys are light and can be easily attached to a diver's belt or placed in the pocket of the diver's buoyancy compensator.

If a large area must be searched and visibility permits, two boats can be used to tow divers with a line stretched between the boats, the number of divers that can be towed can be increased as can the area searched with each pass. Boat searches must also be conducted based on a repeating pattern that can be plotted by compass and chart. All parts of the search must be geographically located and documented for courtroom use. A number of small buoys will be needed to mark the progress of the sweeps being made by the search boat, the smaller buoys will be dropped at a location intersecting the rectangle that forms the perimeter of the search area. These buoys must be larger than the ones the divers carry for marking evidence. The size of the search area may render smaller buoys invisible. The glass and Styrofoam® floats used by fishermen to support their fishing nets work well for marking the route of the search boat. One of these is dropped with enough line and weight to prevent being carried away by waves at each outermost "reach" of the search before direction is reversed and the search continued. By aligning two of these buoys the skipper of the search boat should be able to maintain an overlapping search interval within the rectangular search area.

If the search is being conducted contiguously to a shoreline, it may be simpler to place markers on the shoreline allowing the boat to line up on these markers and use its compass to assist in laying down the search pattern. If these shore markers are laid with the assistance of a transit or similar device, the boat course can be directed by the transit operator. Once the evidence is discovered, it can be marked with a buoy and immediately triangulated by the transit operator.

In water of limited visibility magnetometers or towed sonar arrays, if available, may be used to locate large underwater objects. Sidescan sonar covers a larger area than the handheld or installed echo sounders found in many bass fishing boats. A sophisticated system with a competent operator can sweep shallow waters in 500 hundred foot swaths. In deeper water up to 1200 feet can be examined in each sweep. The sidescan is not affected by weather or visibility. There are a number available in the marketplace beginning at $500.

Proton Magnetometers are affected by focused masses of ferromagnetic metals. Depending on the size of the object sought, or more precisely the amount of ferromagnetic metals used in the manufacture of the item sought will determine how deeply the magnetometer probe must be towed. The strength of the earth's magnetic field is fairly constant within the area surveyed, a significant change in that field is suggestive of a concentrated ferrous mass. Again the size of the iron item sought will determine how close to the bottom the magnetometer probe must be towed. Robert Marx used a proton magnetometer to find the sunken Spanish galleon Maravilla. Although she was buried beneath 25 feet of sand, he was able to locate her and twenty-four other wrecks, anchors, chains, and a fisherman's tackle box (Marx, 1990:123).

If an item sought is below the surface and not of ferrous material, the magnetometer and towed sonar array is of little use. A specialized sonar echo sounder, called a sub bottom profiler, is effective in such searches to a depth of ten feet under the sand. British antiquarians and archaeologists searched in vain for the infamous Mary Rose, sunk in Portsmouth Harbour England in 1545. Search efforts had concentrated in a twelve hundred square foot area known to be the sinking site. Attempts to locate her with sonar and magnetometer had failed. A subbottom profiler revealed her location beneath ten feet of silt and mud, within that 1200 foot search area.

Although most police agencies may not have underwater sensoring devices, often military or oceanographic organizations will be willing to assist in a search operation. When searching for items such as large aircraft or sunken vessels a compass may reflect the change in the earth's magnetic field resulting from interference from a large metal mass.

Historically, the most common method of boat search was the towed cable search. This technique is only effective in waters with unlittered and geologically undisturbed bottoms. The cable search is applicable in those situations in which large evidentiary items are sought. This method employs two boats towing a heavily weighted cable between them. The length of the cable will determine the scope of each pass. The size of the boats and the motors driving them will limit the length of the cable that can be towed. It will be apparent when a large obstruction is snagged. As the boats retrieve the played-out cable they will eventually back over the snagged obstacle. Once the item is directly below, a diver can be dispatched to mark the evidence. Most of the shipwrecks in the Baltic and North seas have been discovered utilizing this method. The most recent discovery of note was the Galliot found in 120 feet of water near the Borsto Islands in the Baltic Sea. The ship, sunk between 1700 and 1710, was found intact and upright. In the cold, impenetrable Baltic waters, divers found, in the main cabin, the skeleton of a man, enameled snuffboxes, pocket watches, and clothing (Falcon-Barker, 1964).

Search Patterns

In water of limited visibility or irregular bottom structure, searching may be done in the water by divers utilizing a search pattern. In black water diving, lines must be sunk to which divers can hold while conducting a search by feel, handheld sonar, or metal detector. Handheld sonar can be used in any of the search patterns described below. A sonar unit will emit a beep when it senses an item protruding up from the bottom. As the diver descends, the beep will be louder. It would be helpful if these devices also produced a vibration that increases in intensity as the object being sensed draws closer. Once an item is sensed, that location should be marked with a buoy before the search is interrupted so that if the item sensed is not the object sought, the search can continue at the point the item was first sensed.

The same approach should be used when the diver is operating a hand held metal detector. Most detectors use dials, and audible signals to assist in locating metal. It would prove helpful for these devices also to have a vibratory component to assist in searches involving limited visibility.

Often low visibility and no visibility searches are conducted without the assistance of electronic devices. Hand searches are like crawling through visually impenetrable mud wearing gloves, attempting to identify by touch the things the hand grasps or touches. All the senses focus on the hand and fingers and the sense of touch heightens to the point that a diver wearing gloves can touch a pull tab from a beer or soft drink can and without picking it up tell that it is a pull tab. A search must be undertaken with diligence and perseverance. A systematic search method will prevent duplication of efforts and facilitate documentation and in court testimony.

The nature and scope of the search will be determined by the offense, existing current, tidal conditions, water depth, visibility, wind direction, and known bottom structure. It is the recovery team leader's responsibility to determine, based on the relevant variables, which search pattern to employ.

Search patterns vary and have different attributes enabling them to address different search requirements, but all search patterns should have certain basic attributes:

1. The pattern is to begin at a predetermined point, have predetermined midpoints and changes of direction, ending at a predetermined location or upon discovery of the item sought.
2. Includes communication from surface personnel to searchers through line signals or voice communication.

3. Allows the searcher to deploy buoys to mark points of interest or evidence.
4. Is simple.
5. Effectively uses divers and resources.
6. Allows for safe support of the diver or divers.

Most searches involve a surface component (line tender) and a diver or divers. All divers should be competent in line tending. As a team the diver provides the labor and the tender, provides the direction and support. The tender is the divers lifeline. The tender is responsible for keeping notes of the dive as to location, direction, duration, and depth. In those instances when a diver is unable to determine air consumption and depth, it will fall to the tender to provide that information. Each tender will need a compass, timepiece, flotation device, and notepad. A compass is necessary to record search direction and termination points and a watch is essential to approximate air consumption and time at depth.

Line Signals

Prior to every recovery effort, all participants should review line signals. Departments often evolve their own line language. At the beginning, line talk should be kept simple to avoid confusion. A standard set of simple signals would include the following:

1. One tug is not generally used in order to avoid confusing a request for an inadvertent snag.
2. Two tugs by the line tender means to change direction, and take the previously agreed amount of line. By the diver, means to allow more line to be taken.
3. Three tugs by the diver means an item has been located.
4. Four or more tugs is a distress signal.

Random Search

Although not a pattern at all, inserting a number of divers at a search site and having them cast about within that area, may prove successful in small search areas with maximum visibility. Not generally seen as artful or strategic, it may render a positive result quickly. In clear water with bottoms layered with sediment it is important not to dive too deeply thereby agitating that sediment and prohibiting a subsequent patterned search, if the random search is unsuccessful.

Sweep Search

This is the most commonly employed search method, for searches conducted contiguous to an accessible shoreline, bridge, dock, pier, or in a river whose current requires a line stretched across the river. The diver swims, tethered to the tender by a quarter inch polypropelene line, in everbroadening arcs. The tender line remains taut and the tender and diver remain in continuous communication through line signals. The farthest reaches of the arcs should be determined by the tender using landmarks, placed buoys, or compass bearing. The terminus of the arcs should be recorded in the tender's notebook and included in a sketch of the search site and search pattern. When the bottom drops quickly it may be best to employ a parallel pattern to avoid running the diver into the shore and reduce the number of times the ear must equalize pressure because of rapid or numerous changes in depth. Underwater obstacles can be addressed in one of three fashions:

1. Raise the line tender.
2. Conduct the search up to the obstacle and begin again on the other side of the obstacle.
3. Place a flotation device in the middle of the tender line, thereby raising the line off the bottom.

Parallel Search

When the area to be searched is relatively free of obstruction, and close to the shoreline, this pattern allows lengthy passes along the shoreline, extending outward. Markers should be placed on the shore at the farthest reaches of the pattern. The tender moves back and forth between these two markers paralleling the diver. At the furthest reaches of the pattern, two tugs on the tender line communicates to the diver that it is time to return to the direction from which he came but at a slightly greater distance to the shoreline. The amount of line fed to the diver on each direction change has been predetermined depending upon visibility or an arms distance for hand searches.

In this search it is necessary for the diver to hold the tender line in the inside hand, i.e., the hand closest to the shore. Upon changing direction the outside hand will become the inside hand. The turn should be made by directing the head shoreward, thereby making an inside turn and avoiding entangling the tender line with tank or fins.

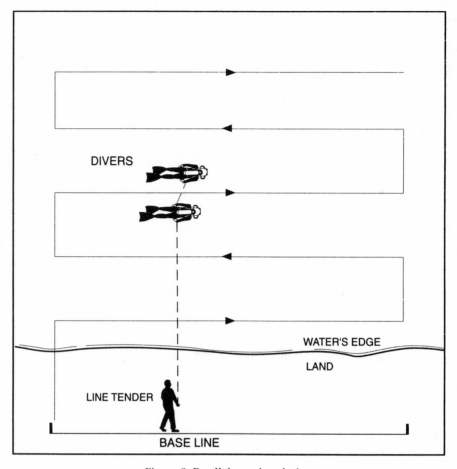

DIVERS

WATER'S EDGE

LAND

LINE TENDER

BASE LINE

Figure 3. Parallel search technique.

Circular Search

This is generally a boat-based search. In areas not susceptible to
search using a land based line tender, the tender works from a boat. In
shallow waters the line tender is at the center of the circle in a boat,
feeding line to the diver(s) who swim in a 360 degree circle, stop and
change direction. At the point where the direction is changed, additional
line is fed to the diver(s). The line tender directs the search using a
landmark, an anchored buoy, or a compass bearing for the change of
direction point. Changing direction is less disorienting than swimming
in concentric circles and does not require the tender to continue turning
in circles.

In deeper water the line may have to be fed to the diver from an

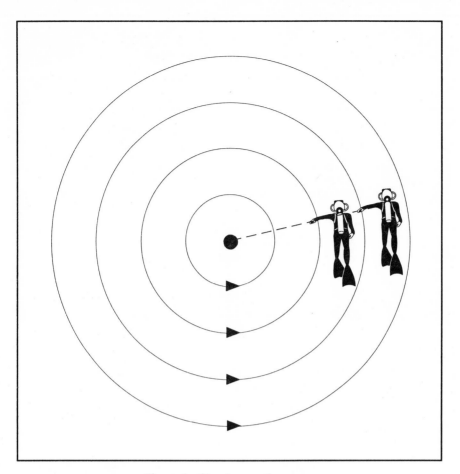

Figure 4a. Circular search pattern.

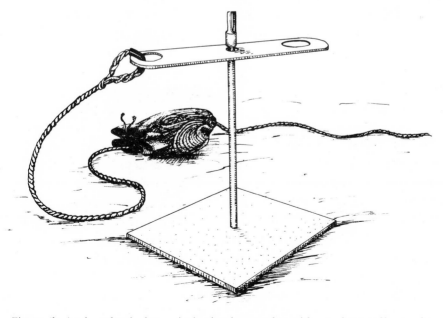

Figure 4b. Anchored swivel to assist in circular searches without a boat or line tender.

anchored swivel fed by the surface line tender. Departments have built a variety of anchored swivel devices, but the device pictured in Figure 6 will work well. It should be noted that when employing an underwater anchored swivel, the diver should continue to change direction at the completion of each circuit to avoid fouling the tender line around the anchor line.

Circular searches can be conducted without a boat, using a submerged diver as the tender and center of the search pattern. Using compass bearings the "anchored" diver can direct the search and the needed directional changes.

Snag Search

The snag search is not a search pattern but a search method. This technique can be used with an arch pattern, parallel pattern, or circular pattern. Just as in boat-towed snag searches, the size of the item sought and the presence of submerged obstructions determines the applicability of this procedure. The value of this technique is that it allows large areas to be searched in a short period of time. The tender allows more line to the diver than he would in a hand or vision search.

Grid Search

In clear water this is a search that can be conducted without a tender. Using compass bearings the diver can direct the course of his own search. When conducting a compass search it is practical to use two divers, one maintaining compass heading and the other conducting the visible search of the bottom. The furthest reaches of the search should be marked by buoy so that the next pass is at a consistent distance from the last pass. This search method is also used by boats towing sled riding divers.

River Search

River searches can be especially tedious when significant current is present. Depending on the intensity of the current, it may well be that a search is impossible. In currents of manageable proportions, to be determined by the team leader, it may be necessary to provide the "river diver" line-based assistance. This procedure depends on the availability of land-based anchor points on opposite sides of the river. The anchorages must be of sufficient strength to withstand 500 pounds of pressure. A line must be extended from one anchor point to the other. The line

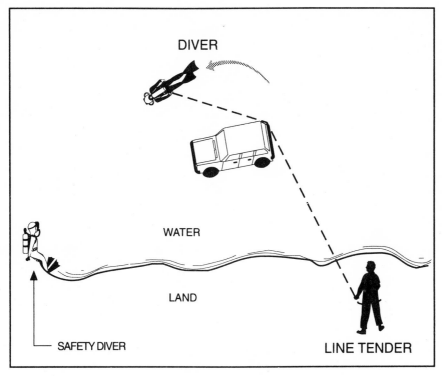

DIVER

WATER

LAND

SAFETY DIVER

LINE TENDER

Figure 5. Snag search procedure.

should be pulled taut, using mechanical devices if necessary, e.g., vehicle, fence stretcher, winch. A sled (or sleds) is (are) attached to the traversing line through a carrabiner or other device that will allow the sled line to be pulled back and forth across the river as well as allow the divers to feed line up and down river. The tender lines, one on each side of the river, are attached to the carrabiner. Once the primary lines have been set, a secondary line, downstream of the area being worked, needs to be anchored in a similar fashion. The secondary line will serve as a safety device and as a method for divers to exit the water by simply letting the river carry them to the secondary line. The secondary line should be angled to the flow of the river instead of perpendicular, allowing easier exit. Swift water searches are dangerous and should be avoided. If unavoidable, maximum safety precautions must be taken.

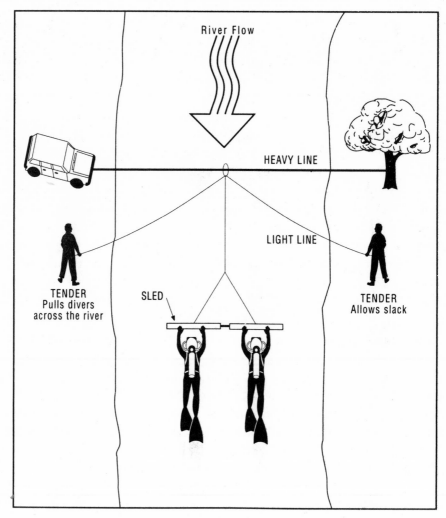

Figure 6. Technique for conducting a search in strong river current.

Relocating the Search Site

It may be necessary to return to the search site on a day other than the one upon which the search was begun. It may be necessary to continue searching on subsequent days, in which case the accurate plotting of the previous day's search pattern will prevent beginning anew or guessing where the search left off. Once evidence has been found it may take days to completely process and recover the evidence, in which case it will be necessary to return to the precise location. Floating buoys left unattended may disappear. In order to return to the appropriate spot, it must be permanently marked for relocation. If the search is accompanied by a transit operator the location can be preserved by triangulation. Often divers will attempt to use compass bearings to triangulate their positions. Although subject to significant margins of error depending on the distance of the objects used for triangulation, in many instances it is all that is available. When using a compass to locate a site, the objects from which bearings are taken should be greater than 30 degrees apart. When plotted on a map, these bearings should return the team to the general location. In addition to the compass triangulation, a buoy should be sunk four or five feet below the surface at the exact spot to facilitate rapid reacquisition of the search site or evidence being recovered. For those agencies that have the resources, there are submersible transponders that emit a signal that can be picked up on handheld sonar. Obviously, such a transponder makes relocating a search site simple. Anyone competent in navigation skills should have no trouble in plotting the location of the search site using typical navigational instruments and shoreside landmarks. There are numerous commercial hunting and military, handheld range finders that are available. Although these devices are not as accurate as an instrument stabilized on a tripod and calibrated for accuracy, they are a reasonable addition to the equipment inventory.

Searches conducted out of the sight of land pose an additional problem. Typical navigational abilities can only approximately locate the position of a vessel at sea. Sailors using sextants to ascertain their position at sea can only do so with a modicum of accuracy. Radio beacons affixed to various permanent and well-known landmarks allow vessels at sea with radio direction finders (R.D.F.) to triangulate their positions with a degree of certainty. Global Positioning Systems (G.P.S.) use up to twelve satellites accessible globally to anyone with a handheld G.P.S. device to compute positions to an heretofore unattainable degree of accuracy. The G.P.S. can be used on land or at sea. Its only restriction is the ability to receive signals from one of the satellites to which it is calibrated.

Search Summary

In running any of the search patterns described, it is axiomatic that a safety diver be available in the event the diver should encounter problems. The amount of overlap in each search pass is based on visibility or arm length and the size of the item sought. The degree of teamwork and training a team has is generally evident in the set-up, execution and termination of search procedures. Regardless of the search conducted, communication and preparation are the essence of a successful search effort. The preparation begins before a search is requested in the training and readiness maintained by the team and continues right up to the first diver's entry into the water. Communication includes written guidelines and policies that describe and govern the recovery process, tender line language, and accurate documentation of the teams efforts including in court testimony.

REFERENCES

Brylske, A. 1984. *PADI Rescue Diver Manual.* Santa Ana: PADI.

Falcon-Barker, Ted. 1964. *Roman Galley Beneath the Sea.* New York: McGraw-Hill.

Linton, J.S. 1986. *The Dive Rescue Specialist Training Manual.* Fort Collins: Concept Systems, Inc.

Lonsdale, M.V. 1989. *SRT Diver.* Los Angeles: Lonsdale.

Marx, Robert. 1990. *The Underwater Dig.* Houston: Pisces Books.

Teather, R.G. 1983. *The Underwater Investigator.* Fort Collins: Concept Systems, Inc.

Wood, M. 1985. *Dive Control Specialist Handbook.* Fort Collins: Concept Systems, Inc.

Chapter 6

TEMPORAL AND GEOGRAPHICAL
PLOTTING OF EVIDENCE

After the team has located the evidence, the usual procedure is to retrieve it. It is important to remember that the officer recovering the evidence will be responsible for testifying as to the method used in locating, marking, sketching, measuring, photographing, bagging, tagging, and maintaining the chain of custody.

All details pertaining to the dive site must be recorded prior to the recovery of any evidence. The boundaries of the recovery site should be marked with buoys and the entire area plotted on a site chart. This chart must be large enough to contain measurement information about each piece of evidence to be recovered. The methods used to record available information will vary, depending on the size of the recovery area, nature of the items to be recovered, available time, weather conditions, water conditions, visibility, bottom conditions, seriousness of the offense, and manpower demands. Failure to properly mark and record the location of the recovery site may result in:

   a. losing it, in the event more than one dive is necessary;
   b. inability to orient parts of a dismembered or dismantled auto, vessel, airplane, or body. In airline crashes body limbs, arms, hands, legs, and feet may be strewn over the site (Wagner & Froede, 1993:574). Reconstruction of the bodies may require anthropological assistance. Often the fastest way to associate severed body parts with the torso is by recording the location of the body parts relative to the seat or seats the parts were closest to. By referring to the seating chart body parts can be readily associated with the passenger who had been occupying the seat nearest to where the body parts were found;
   c. considerable expense in time and effort in relocating the site and the evidence at the site; or
   d. having the evidence rendered inadmissible at the time of trial.

The most effective method of recordation is photography. Where visibility allows, the camera should be the first piece of equipment on the site. All evidence should be photographed where it is found. After measurement, sketching, and tagging, the evidence should be photographed again, then bagged.

ESTABLISHING A REFERENCE POINT

When discussing measurement methods it is easier to use the metric system. Mathematical operations based on 10 may prove easier than the changing base of inches and feet. However, when testifying it may be necessary to convert meters to inches and feet in order for the jury to understand the distances involved.

When evidence is recovered from a crime scene in a conventional crime, measurement is generally not a problem. There are fixed landmarks from which measurements can be taken. However, underwater there may not be a readily available landmark for a dive team to anchor its measurements. After plotting the recovery area on the site chart, it is generally necessary to establish a point of reference from which measurements can be made. This point should be located at the center of the recovery site, if more than one piece of evidence is to be retrieved, or at the apex of any angle formed by the design of the evidence. A metal stake (painted a high visibility yellow) should be driven deep enough into the bottom to be securely anchored without disturbing the evidence. This pipe can be driven with a handheld metal post driver. Once this pipe is geographically located and plotted on the sight map, all measurements can then be made from the same point.

A reference point must also be located. This can be done by securing a buoy to the stake (underwater reference point) with bearings (bearing point) then recorded from shore. Often bearings are taken using a hand compass and measuring tape. There are a number of other devices that will provide a more accurate measurement. Depending on the budget available, a team may wish to invest in the following:

a. transit
b. carpenter's level (an inexpensive transit with limited horizontal and no vertical measurement functions) or
c. theodolite (a handheld, inexpensive version of a carpenter's level).

Wherever the transit (or other measuring device) is set up (bearing point) on land it must be linked to a permanent landmark, and that measurement must also be recorded. Ultimately, the drawings made from the measurements recorded will allow each piece of evidence to be accurately located from a permanent landmark, i.e.,

a. underwater evidence to underwater reference point;
b. underwater reference point to transit (bearing point); and
c. transit (bearing point) to landmark.

MEASURING EVIDENCE

There are numerous devices available for writing underwater messages. These devices will assist in the tagging and measuring of evidence to be recovered. Once evidence is uncovered, it can be located relative to the underwater reference point. Accurate measurement can be obtained through the use of an underwater compass and measuring tape and recorded on the diver's slate. In addition to the distance from the reference point, the evidence should be tagged with the finders name, date, time, depth, and given a chronological number if more than one item is being processed.

ORIENTING EVIDENCE

Measuring evidence in this fashion does not provide orientation information. Orienting evidence may be as important as locating it in the first place, particularly autos, airplanes and their occupants; vessels and their occupants; debris from fires, explosions, crashes, or collisions. The front, back, and sides of large evidence items can be portrayed by gross (large) measurements from what is recognizably the front back and sides, with those measurements plotted on the site map. However, when dealing with small items of evidence such as coins or weapons, the size of the item makes it impractical to measure to the front, back, and sides. Obviously, the easiest way to orient an item of evidence is to photograph it marking north so the photo can later be oriented with the information plotted on the site map.

A small grid, three meters square, made of plastic pipe and subdivided into ten centimeter squares, with fixed legs six to ten inches long, is invaluable in fixing the position (orientation) of small pieces of evidence such as weapons. Having located the evidence, it is relatively easy to plot its position (orientation) within the grid. First, the grid must be geographically located and plotted, using a buoy or buoys to assist in the plotting. Once the grid is in place, a photograph or tape measurement will allow accurate measurements to the front, back, and sides of the item, thereby orienting the evidence within the grid. The grid can then be plotted on the site map and a separate expanded grid map constructed.

Figure 7. Small measuring/orienting grid with parallax wires.

AZIMUTH

In the event of a recovery site littered with evidence, there are a number of other measuring methods that may prove more useful. A metal circle approximately 12 inches in diameter can be marked with the cardinal points of the compass and then further divided into degrees. Once marked with 360 degrees, the metal circle can be mounted on a

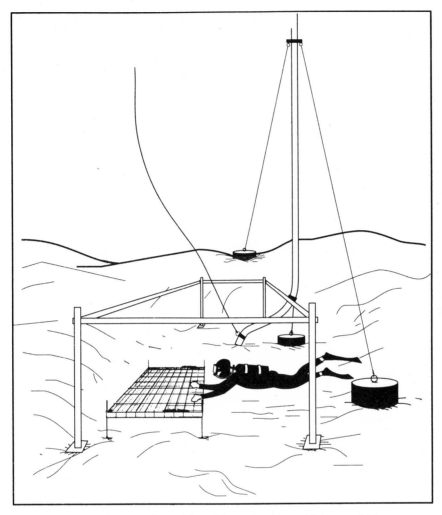

Figure 8. Small measuring grid used in conjunction with large grid frame.

metal rod. North etched on the circle can be oriented with an underwater compass to point north. The rod with the circle mounted upon it can be driven into the bottom structure providing an azimuth circle from which to measure. A buoy is floated from the azimuth circle which allows the underwater location of the azimuth circle to be plotted on the site map. A measuring tape is mounted on the rod above the azimuth circle so that it will turn 360 degrees. When the tape is stretched from the rod of the azimuth circle to the evidence, the diver holding the end of the tape can measure the distance, another diver hovering above the azimuth circle can read and record bearing degrees (Bass G.T., 1968:103).

Figure 9. Azimuth circle and measuring chain.

In many instances, visibility will not allow the use of underwater measuring devices. It should be noted that measurement of the type described above has been used in waters of minimal visibility. Visibility should not be used as an excuse for not measuring. In those instances where time or visibility is limited, measurement can be done from the shore. By locating each piece of evidence with a buoy and placing a buoy in the center of the site, measurements can be had in water of limited visibility. Measurement can be made from the evidence to the buoy placed in the middle of the site and from the centered buoy to a landmark on shore.

PLAN TABLE

The most accurate measurements can be made as a result of underwater triangulation. This method is more accurate but also involves more divers and more time. The tool used for underwater triangulation is a plane table, comprised of a circular base attached to four legs and a sighting device made of tubular metal or plastic. Cross hairs are affixed to each end of the sighting tube. The tube is affixed perpendicularly to a pipe that passes through the base but allows the tube and the pipe to be turned 360 degrees. The base is marked in degrees so that when the sighting tube is turned to sight in on the item to be measured, the tube crosses a marked degree giving the bearing from the plane table (Marx, R.F., 1990:157).

In order to triangulate the position of the evidence being measured, three plane tables are required (one or two can be used, but it triples the time and movement involved). Each plane table should be placed so that

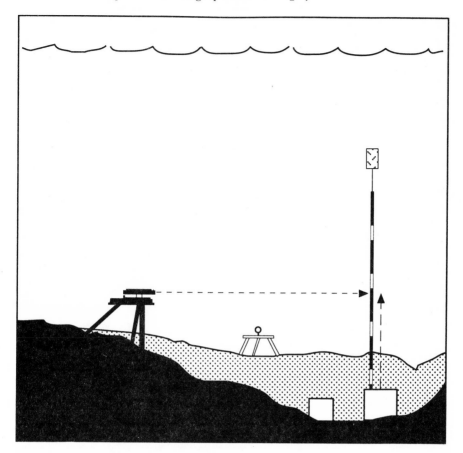

Figure 10. Plane table and floated range pole.

its relative position forms a triangle, the position of each is then plotted on the site chart.

Sightings are made with the assistance of a range pole, a pipe 2 meters long, painted in alternating 10 centimeter sections of yellow and violet. These two colors were selected because water depth affects the colors that can be perceived. Colors are lost as depth increases. The following are the colors lost as depths increase.

    15 ft. Red
    30 ft. Ultraviolet
    60 ft. Yellow and Violet
    100 ft. Blues and Greens

Of course, color loss does not occur all at once, but rather gradually with complete loss occurring at the depths described. The diver with the

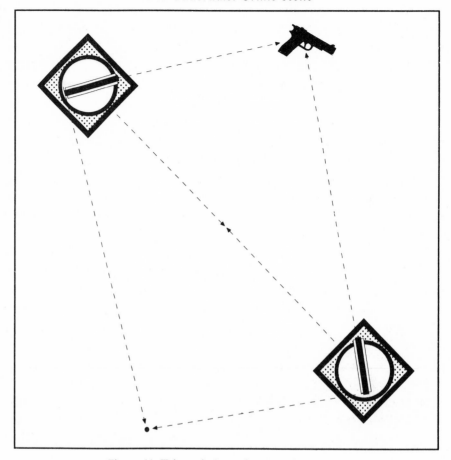

Figure 11. Triangulation using two plane tables.

range pole should position himself over the evidence to be plotted. The range pole can be made neutrally buoyant by attaching a flotation device to the tip of the pole. The diver's sighting through the plane table tube will aim at the range pole and record the degrees bearing from each of the three plane tables by referring to the plane table's azimuth circles. The diver operating the range pole should tag the evidence with a tag previously filled out and applied chronologically, so that the plane table logs for each sighting should describe the evidence sighted by tag number. After triangulation, the bearings logged for each piece of evidence from each plane table can be plotted on the site chart, thereby locating each piece of evidence (Bass, G.F., 1968:99). This method is especially helpful in situations where numerous pieces of evidence are being recovered, as in a plane crash, shipwreck or explosion. In each recovery site that has been plotted into a square or rectangle, visibility permitting, the evidence on that site can be plotted by moving one table one time. With a table in each of three corners of the rectangle, half of that rectangle can be plotted. By moving the table that forms the apex of the first triangle directly across to the opposite corner, the remainder of the rectangle can be plotted.

When using two tables, they must be placed a known distance apart. Instead of a third table, a stake is driven into the seabed at a plotted location. Each sighting then is made to the evidence to be measured and then to the fixed point represented by the stake. When these two measurements are made for each piece of evidence and added to the known distance between the tables the location of each item can be triangulated and plotted.

If the dive sight is in less than 30 feet of water, there is a simpler approach to the plane table concept that can be used. Edmund Scientific manufactures a carpenter's construction level that contains a compact diode-type laser so that the laser beam extends the reference of the level to the distance of the laser (100 ft.). The laser projects a beam of light from the end of the level producing a eye safe, eye visible laser beam. Using this construction level by placing it on top of the plane table absent the sighting tube would allow bearings to be taken on the survey rod by laser beam. This level is not designed for underwater operations and cannot withstand more than one atmosphere of pressure. This device can be employed on recovery sites in water depths less than 30 feet where visibility allows.

Providing that the plane table is level, both elevation (height) and horizontal datum can be obtained using plane tables. Elevation measurements can be obtained by plotting the depth of the sighting device on one plane table. Knowing the surface water level allows the plane table to be located vertically. Once the table has been vertically located elevation data can be obtained for any evidence on the recovery site. By recording where the cross hairs (or laser beam) line up on the range pole, elevations can be recorded along with horizontal data. In order to obtain underwater elevations three measurements must be had;

  1. water depth at the plane table site
  2. altitude of the waters' surface at the time elevations are taken, and
  3. length of range pole (incrementally).

Plane tables, first used during the excavation of the Byzantine shipwreck at Yassi Ada and later employed on the two wrecks near Methome in Greece, have the advantages of being extremely inexpensive, for the components can be made of items readily at hand. Their use depends on clear water, however, and since they require the work of several divers at a time, they are time-consuming.

AQUALEVEL

Traditionally, divers have measured elevation by using what is often referred to as a water or aqua level. A length (depending on visibility and site size) of half inch transparent garden hose is filled with air (breathing from the regulator into the hose and back until the hose is filled). One end of the hose is placed at a known underwater elevation (usually the highest object on the site). The hose, which is buoyant because of the air will contain air and water. The point at which the air and water meet is held on the known underwater elevation. The hose, which is buoyant because of the entrapped air, forms an arc, and the opposite end is held by another diver holding a range pole over the evidence to be measured. The position of the air water interface on the range pole then indicates the elevation difference between the two points. This method is useful in measuring elevations of large objects.

The easiest way to determine elevations is by using a depth gauge. As technology evolves, digital depth gauges are being continuously refined. It should not be long before depth gauges are sensitive enough to measure depths to the centimeter.

GRID SYSTEM

Highly accurate horizontal data can also be obtained by placing pipe squares (grids), two meters to the side, over the recovery site. Each grid has four adjustable telescoping pipe legs, one in each corner. The adjustable legs allow the grid to be placed on the bottom over the evidence and leveled. The total number of grids placed will vary depending on the size of the site. The length of the telescoping legs can be varied depending on the size of the evidence in question.

These grids can be made to interlock by placing each adjacent grid on two of the legs holding the grid already in place. These interlocking grids form manageable areas for minute examination and measurement of whatever evidence falls within the grid. Once the grids have been

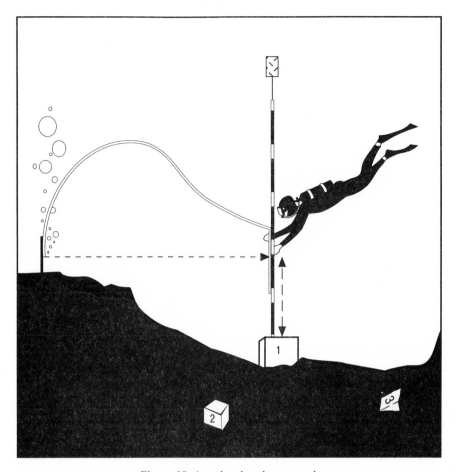

Figure 12. Aqualevel and range pole.

plotted measurements can then be taken within the grids. The pipes forming the frame of the grid can be painted in alternating 10 centimeter bands assisting in measurement. The dimensions of the grids and legs should be calculated and built keeping in mind the method whereby they will be transported to the site. PVC tubing may be used but will not provide the bottom stability of galvanized metal. The design of the grids should be such that they can be taken apart for ease of transportation. Equipment used in salt water will constantly resist efforts at dismantling. It is possible to further subdivide the grid by tying wire or rope to the corresponding 10 centimeter marks, thereby relegating examination and measurements to a 10 centimeter square area.

One of the first uses of a grid system for underwater recording was by George Bass at Yassi Ada, Turkey. Dr. Bass was attempting to recover the

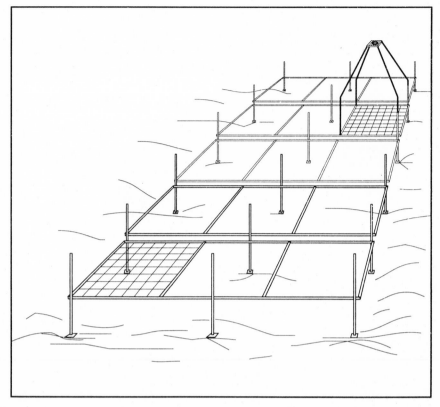

Figure 13. Interlocking grids placed on an expanded excavation site: note the movable photo tower.

remains of a Byzantine wreck located in 120 feet of water. The wreck lay in an area 30 feet by 70 feet but covered by seaweed. Seaweed had to be removed before the visible artifacts could be tagged and the site covered with three meter grid squares on which wires were strung 10 centimeters apart. Teams of divers made measurements of what they saw in each 10 centimeter square. Dissatisfied with the time involved in making these measurements, he discovered that an accurate photographic record of each grid taken at a stable constant height would produce measurements that were as accurate as hand measurements but that were less labor intensive and time consuming. In order for the camera to be held at a constant and stable level he had built a 13 foot platform that bolted to a grid at the four corners and provided an inexpensive tower from which pictures could be taken. The photographs taken were from the same height and angle so that any distortion remained constant and could be compensated for. The panorama produced by this photographic record was transferred to a scale drawing and provided accurate measurements (Marx, 1990:162).

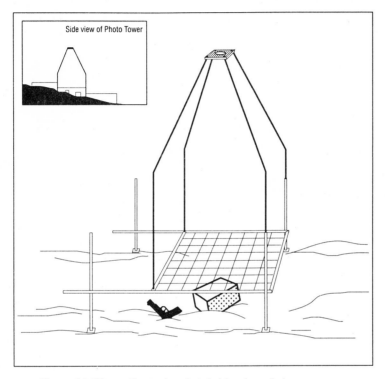

Figure 14. Three-dimensional and side view of photo tower.

PHOTOGRAMMETRY

Using a photo tower can produce horizontal measurements but if elevations are important a photo tower used as described will not provide elevations. Dimitri Rebikoff has devised a method whereby a shipwreck can be accurately measured horizontally and vertically photogrammetrically. His method does away with the need for hand measurements altogether. A bar is floated above the site at a constant height. A camera designed to take stereo pictures is slid along the bar and a series of overlapping pictures is taken. The matched photos are measured for differences in parallax with digital measuring devices thereby locating each item visible in the photograph (Williams, 1972:220).

Not all recovery sites lend themselves to all the measurement methods described. Not all cases warrant expenditures of time and money, not all departments have budgets allowing for sophisticated measurement or photographic activities. Time, weather, current, and visibility will undoubtedly play an important role in the recovery process and the measurement employed. It should be emphasized that limited visibility, time, or budget are not excuses for abandoning all attempts at measurement.

REFERENCES

Bass, G.B. 1968. *Archaeology Under Water.* New York: Frederick A. Praeger.
Blackman, D.J. 1973. *Marine Archaeology.* London: Martin Robertson.
Cleator, P.E. 1973. *Underwater Archaeology.* New York: Holt, Rinehart, and Winston.
Marx, R.F. 1990. *The Underwater Dig.* Houston: Pisces Books.
Wagner & Froede. 1993. Mass Disasters. In *Medicolegal Investigation of Death,* 3rd. ed. Werner U. Sitz. Springfield: Charles C Thomas.
Williams, J.C.C. 1972. Underwater surveying by Simple Graphic Photogrammetry With Obliques. *Underwater Archaeology: A Nascent Discipline.* Paris: United Nations.
UNESCO Publication. 1972. *Underwater Archaeology.* Paris: United Nations.

Chapter 7

UNDERWATER EXCAVATION

In most police underwater recovery operations, retrieving the evidence is simply a matter of lifting it to the surface by hand, float, or winch. In some instances, recovering evidence may require removing sediment from on top of the item to be recovered. This chapter will deal with those recovery operations that require removal of overburden (successive layers of sediment sometimes measured in meters) before evidence can be wholly recovered.

Historically, evidentiary items that were partially buried and too large to be cleared by hand were simply winched to the surface in whole or in pieces. Whatever portions were left behind were considered unimportant or unsalvageable. Field archaeologists have long employed excavation techniques that have allowed them to recover entire cities and the remains of the occupants of those cities without loss. Marine archaeologists have recovered entire vessels and their cargoes using similar techniques. The many problems involved in excavation fall into two categories: the recording of each element by mapping, sketching, and photography, and the work of extraction. The main difficulty of underwater archaeology lies in the necessity of accurately recording the position of each object and element of the site, so as to prepare as complete a survey as possible of all aspects recovered (Dumas, 1972:155). The main task of law enforcement underwater recovery operations should be no less.

The excavation is a time consuming methodical process. Obviously such efforts are warranted in only the most extreme and serious cases. Proper use of underwater excavation procedures requires considerable planning, patience, and dedication. If the evidence buried is important it is best to work carefully on a small area than to risk destroying evidence through hasty unplanned sorties against the entire site. If the recovered item is to have evidentiary value, strict archaeological procedure must be employed in mapping and recording archaeological information.

Regardless of the size of the excavation site, the number of persons actively involved should be composed of pairs, both above and below the surface. Safety is a preeminent consideration and requires that a prospective safety diver be prepared to enter the water at all times. In prolonged excavations, communication devices should be employed or a diver used as a "runner." The length of time each diver can spend in the water will be determined by the depth of the site and duration of each dive. There is a greater margin of safety in using dive computers rather than the standard U.S. Navy dive tables for recording depth time and nitrogen absorption. One member of each pair should be equipped with a dive computer.

When working at depth decompression stops need to be stationed and scheduled. The estimated length of time needed to excavate and the depth of the site will determine the number of dive pairs necessary to maximize each pair's dive time in the water. With divers burning off residual nitrogen from deep sites, divers may spend more time on the surface than they do in the water. Lengthy surface intervals require more divers, if the intent is to keep divers in the water during daylight hours.

The surface team is generally more physically active than the divers. The surface team is responsible for operating the excavation equipment, repositioning the boat, raising excavated items, maintaining the site map, recording and packaging recovered items.

In situations requiring excavation, each item uncovered should be photographed, located geographically, oriented, tagged, and retrieved. To this end it may be necessary to use the grid system described in an earlier chapter. When using a grid with one set of lines stretched within the frame it is necessary to use a plumb bob to assure that the view being reproduced and the measurements being made are directly perpendicular to the item of interest. A method that can be employed to avoid the use of a plumb bob is to construct a grid one meter or two meters square with adjustable legs which should allow for leveling the grid and lay over it a second "parallax" grid of the same dimensions. This second grid should have lines stretched exactly along the same plane but five centimeters above the lines of the grid upon which the "parallax grid" rests. By looking down upon the item being measured until the lines of both grids appear as one, the diver is directly over the object within the grid and can record what is seen.

Instead of sketching what the diver observes, a Plexiglas® plate can be placed over the grid and the item below can be traced directly onto the

Plexiglas. Once the Plexiglas plate has been filled in, the plate can be returned topside and the items traced can be transferred onto a site map.

Land excavations have long used mechanical as well as hand methods of removing overburden. Frontend loaders, bulldozers, shovels, sifting screens, wheelbarrows, dental picks, trowels, tooth brushes, paint brushes, dustpans, and brooms have long been part of the field archaeologist's tool kit. None of these are effective for underwater excavation. Nonetheless, underwater excavation should be easier although more time consuming. The bottom structures are generally looser, and the materials of which they are formed are approximately half as dense. Moreover, the water itself can be effectively employed to scoop out or sweep away the soil, by means of three simple tools: the air-lift, water-jet, and the prop-wash.

In operations involving the movement of large amounts of overburden, it is self-defeating to begin removing the overburden from the entire site. As removal progresses the amount of overburden removed may make room for additional sediment from adjacent areas already partially excavated. To avoid replacing old sediment with new it is generally helpful to trench the site allowing a repository for shifting sediment. The depth of the trench is determined by the depth of the artifact being recovered. Trenching is best accomplished by use of an air-lift in sand and a water-jet or a surface operated grab bucket for trenching in mud.

AIR-LIFT

Divers cannot shovel dirt into wheelbarrows. The airlift is the "shovel" of underwater recovery. It was first used by Jacques Yves Cousteau during his excavation of the Roman wreck at Grand Congloue island near Marseilles (Bass, 1968:125). The air-lift consists of a metal, rubber or semirigid plastic tube to whose lower end is connected a hose. The hose is connected to an air compressor into which compressed air is pumped. As the air enters near the bottom it rises to the surface in the form of bubbles. As the bubbles near the surface, they get bigger because of the decreasing pressure. The rising action causes suction, a vacuum cleaner type effect at the mouth of the tube. The sucking action pulls in water as well as sand, mud, gravel and other material small enough to fit through the tubing.

The hose providing air to the lift should have a valve that can be opened and closed in graduated steps, allowing the diver using the lift to regulate the amount of air from the compressor to the lift tube. By reducing the compressed air supply, the diver can regulate the severity of the suction at the lift tube mouth. It should be remembered that any evidence lifted will not be mapped as to location; it is therefore wise to use the air-lift as a method to remove dirt and not to retrieve evidence. Fanning the sediment into the air-lift reduces the likelihood of lifting items of evidence that should be measured and photographed once unburdened. Small items of evidence may be inadvertently lifted. The air-lift can discharge the water, sediment, and debris onto the surface, or it can discharge under water; in both cases some filtering system is necessary to catch any items which may have entered the tube.

Water surface conditions may prohibit securing the lift tube to a barge or boat. Any raising of the boat by water action will result in a concomitant rise of the working end of the tube. In such instances it may be necessary to float the top of the tube below the surface of the water, having only the compressor hose secured to the boat or barge.

The air pressure used in an air-lift must be at least one atmosphere (33 feet per square inch) greater than the surrounding ambient water pressure. The size of the compressor hose and air compressor are determined by the lift tube's diameter and the depth of the excavation. Following is a chart indicating the diameter of the tube and hose required at various depths and the amount of air pressure and volume of air needed to work efficiently.

Water weighs 14.7 pounds per square inch at sea level to a depth of 33 feet. Every 33 feet of depth thereafter water pressure increases by 14.7 pounds per square inch. The air-lift cannot be used effectively in water less than 33 feet deep, because there is no pressure differential at that depth.

The hose leading from the compressor to the lift tube should be attached six inches above the tube mouth. The hose can be any type of low pressure hose. The type and capacity of compressor required will be determined by the volume and pressure deemed necessary for underwater operations in a specific geographical area. Agencies need to be familiar with the range of depths in areas wherein underwater recovery operations are most likely to occur.

Safety considerations will generally restrict the lift tube diameter to six inches. A larger diameter can move more overburden, but it is more difficult to control and may cause injury to fingers or limbs if placed in proximity to the mouth of the lift tube.

Marine archaeologists have learned that mud and sand can be cut

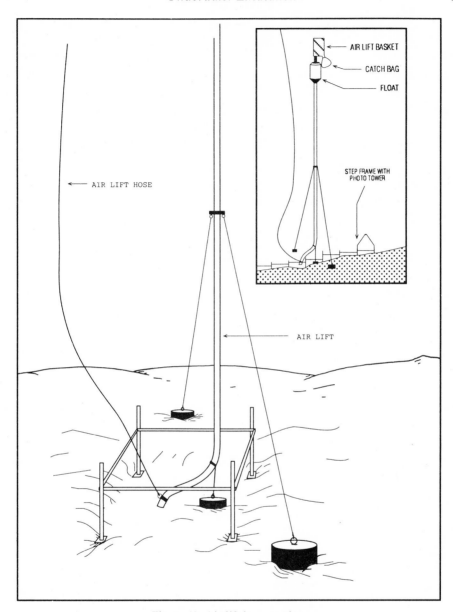

Figure 15. Air lift in operation.

away from the item overburdened without moving the item itself by means of currents formed by short, well-directed sweeps of the hand, displacing clouds of silt and sand.

Airlift diameter	Hose diameter	Maximum depth	Air volume in cubic ft. per minute	Air pressure in pounds per square inch (minimum)
3 inch	½ inch	33 feet	20–40 cfm	45 psi
3 inch	½ inch	66 feet	30–50 cfm	60 psi
3 inch	½ inch	99 feet	40–60 cfm	75 psi
4 inch	¾ inch	33 feet	30–50 cfm	45 psi
4 inch	¾ inch	66 feet	40–60 cfm	60 psi
4 inch	¾ inch	99 feet	59–70 cfm	75 psi
6 inch	1¼ inch	33 feet	75–100 cfm	45 psi
6 inch	1¼ inch	66 feet	100–125 cfm	60 psi
6 inch	1¼ inch	99 feet	125–150 cfm	75 psi

Metric Equivalents
3 inch = 7.62 centimeters
4 inch = 10.16 centimeters
6 inch = 15.24 centimeters
45 psi = 3 bars
60 psi = 4 bars
75 psi = 5 bars

½ inch = 1.27 centimeters
¾ inch = 1.9 centimeters
1¼ inch = 3.18 centimeters

WATER-JET

The water-jet is a high pressure fire hose with a valve that can be regulated for delicate work, for removing sand masses or for cutting hard mud. Heavy substances cannot be driven far and after being cut loose may have to be further removed by use of an air-lift. The water-jet is subject to considerable recoil and must therefore be counterweighted or anchored. This is a tool of tremendous power and can cause damage to divers as well as the recovery site. The water-jet is a tool to be used with great discretion.

PROP-WASH

In shallow sites or sites of heavy overburden not in excess of 35 feet, a prop-wash is an effective excavating tool. First used by Chesapeake Bay oyster fishermen to blow away sediment covering their oyster beds, it has rapidly gained a reputation as a valuable excavation tool. It consists of an elbow-shaped aluminum or stainless steel tube several inches larger in diameter than the propellers of the vessel upon which it is to be used. The tube is attached to the transom of the vessel in such a way that the turbulence created by the propeller is directed toward the bottom. It is necessary to construct a wire mesh guard around the propellers to prevent the divers from accidentally being sucked into the propellers.

The vessel upon which the prop-wash is mounted must be kept stationary when the prop-wash is being used. This can be accomplished with anchor pairs set fore and aft, with emphasis on the aft placement. Depending on the length of anchor lines and the size of the site being cleared, the vessel can be moved by loosening anchor lines aft and taking up forward anchor lines without the vessel actually being under weigh.

The effective depth to which a prop-wash can be used is dependent upon the size and speed of the propeller. A propeller two feet in diameter can be used to depths of 35 feet. Vessels with propellers of five foot diameters can successfully move sediment down to 75 feet. In 20 feet of water a prop-wash two to three feet in diameter can excavate a hole 20 feet in diameter and 15 feet deep in a matter of minutes.

The successful use of a prop-wash is dependent upon controlling how fast the screws (propellers) turn. The control of the prop-wash is affected by the boat operator, but the speed and duration are controlled by the divers. It takes time and practice to develop the skill and trust necessary to work below a vessel with turning screws, but without a visual perspective of the work being done by the prop-wash, that work can easily become damage.

LIFT BAGS

Working in water has a definite advantage when it comes time to recover items from off the bottom. The lift bag is a device that avoids the need for heavy lifting equipment, barges, and winches. Lift bags are simple in design and operation, coming in sizes that will accommodate most needs. Resembling a jellyfish, they are made of air tight, rip resistant material with lift lines attached to an opening at the bottom. The lines trailing the bag are attached to the object that is to be lifted. Air is injected into the bag making it buoyant. Bags of sufficient size and confirmation can be inflated to lift an automobile. As the object being lifted rises the pressure on the lift bag decreases as well as the pressure on the air contained in the bag, it therefore becomes necessary to "dump" air as the item rises to avoid shooting the item skyward when the bag reaches the surface.

For large items, the least expensive lifting device is a fifty-five gallon drum to which twisted wire cables are attached. The drums are sunk near the item to be lifted and filled with air from a topside compressor. Once the object reaches the surface it can be towed to shallow water where it can be more easily retrieved.

The lifting operation is not begun until the evidence has been photographed, measured, mapped, tagged, and if possible, packaged. Most evidence will deteriorate less rapidly if packaged in the water, with water in the package. Items packed in seawater should be moved as quickly as possible to freshwater storage until preservation treatment can be started. Packaging small evidentiary items in water awaiting preservation procedures is not a problem, but it may take some imagination and ingenuity to water pack larger items.

PRESERVING NONHUMAN EVIDENCE

Once an object has been recovered, it becomes necessary to address the potential deterioration of the item as a result of its immersion. Obviously, items recovered from saltwater are at a greater risk than items recovered from freshwater. Some items such as gold and precious stones require little treatment other than a washing in distilled water to remove soluble salts. Most glass is not affected by saltwater immersion and simply requires a freshwater cleansing to remove sand and salts. Silver and iron undergo an electrolytic change in saltwater that causes silver to change to silver sulfide and iron to iron oxide. To remove corrosion from ferrous metals (firearms), two methods can be used: electrochemical or electrolytic reduction.

Electrochemical reduction involves a bath of 10 percent sodium hydroxide and 90 percent water into which the corroded item is placed. The length of the immersion in the sodium hydroxide bath varies from four to eight weeks, depending on the size of the item that is being treated. The bath is renewed and zinc plates are added, creating an active chemical froth which, over a five-week period, should remove any remaining corrosion.

Electrolytic reduction is an electrochemical process involving an electrolyte solution of 10 percent caustic soda in water sufficient to cover the item. The corroded item is suspended in the solution by copper wires attached to insulated conducting rods across the mouth of the steel vessel in which the bath is contained. The vat is connected to the positive side of a twelve volt, direct current power source and the rods are connected to the negative side of the same power source. When the power source is activated the corrosion will gradually disappear. The power source must be sufficient to generate five amperes for each 25 square inches of surface of the item being cleansed.

After either method, the ferrous object should be immersed in distilled water for two weeks and then dried in an oven at 200 degrees Fahrenheit for twenty-four hours. If the item is to be subjected to tests such as ballistic firing, it should be tested then packaged in a corrosion resistant medium such as oil cloth, cosmoline, gun grease, or covered in paraffin. Organic materials such as textiles and paper should be examined while wet and detailed pictures taken, then allowed to air dry.

DATA COLLECTION

After excavation, temporal and geographical location and recovery, sufficient information should have been obtained to begin formulating the data to be included in the recovery operation report. Included in the initial drafting of the report should be:

1. the exact location of the search site
2. the method employed in locating the search site
3. mapping/charting methodology
4. maps made
5. evidence inventory by tag and description
6. recovery method used
7. equipment used
8. photo log
9. personnel involved and roles performed by each
10. weather conditions
11. current and tidal information
12. visibility
13. depth
14. time from beginning of the operation until the operation was terminated

15. dive logs
16. vessel logs.

All the tools of the underwater investigator are presently in use by marine archaeologists. There is no need to reinvent the wheel. College level courses in marine archaeology and underwater excavation work could prove an invaluable asset to the underwater recovery team diver. A summer spent in pursuit of such education would be well spent and multiply its impact by sharing the experience with other team members. An agency that wished to strive for excellence in its recovery operations would be well advised to provide in-service training credit for any such endeavor.

REFERENCES

Bass, G. F. 1968. *Ancient Peoples and Places: Archaeology Under Water.* New York: Frederick A. Praeger.

Blackman, D. J. 1973. *Marine Archaeology.* London: Heinemann.

Cleator, P.E. 1973. *Underwater Archaeology.* New York: Praeger.

Dumas, F. 1972. Problems of Wreck Diving. *Underwater Archaeology: A Nascent discipline.* United Nations Educational, Scientific and Cultural Organization. Switzerland: Unesco.

Dumas, F. 1962. *Deep-Water Archaeology.* London: Oxford University Press.

Erickson, E. and Tregel, S. 1966. *Conservation of Iron Recovered from the Sea.* Copenhagen: Authors.

Marx, R.F. 1990. *The Underwater Dig.* Houston: Gulf.

Muckelroy, K. 1980. *Archaeology Under Water.* New York: McGraw-Hill.

Organ, R.N. 1961. The Conservation of Fragile Metallic Objects. *Studies in conservation.* 6:135–36 (November).

Taylor, J. P. 1965. *Marine Archaeology.* London: F.T. Goulding.

Throckmorton, P. 1969. *Shipwrecks and Archaeology.* Boston: Houghton Mifflin.

Wilkes, B. S. 1971. *Nautical Archaeology.* New York: Doubleday.

Chapter 8

HANDLING EVIDENCE

I n deciding what to do with evidence, it would be helpful to understand the locus of potential forensic information. After expending
considerable time and effort in locating and recovering underwater
evidence, it would be disappointing to destroy residual or transient
forensic evidence because of carelessness or ignorance.

AUTOMOBILES

Stolen autos are commonly retrieved from various waterways. Stolen
auto recovery is such an integral part of underwater recovery operations
that it has become standard procedure to presume that a submerged
vehicle is a stolen vehicle. This perspective leads to the possible destruction of evidence if the vehicle was used in a crime or if a crime was
committed within the vehicle. Human remains that repose within the
vehicle will be unnecessarily thrown about the interior along with their
possessions.

Most agencies place a hooked cable around the axle of the submerged
vehicle and then have it winched to shore by a tow truck or barge. If the
vehicle has filled with water the pressure of the water within the vehicle
against the windows will burst the windows. Anything within the vehicle
that floats will be jettisoned with the water, including clothing, paper,
plastic or items contained in plastic, all of which may have provided
information about a crime that was committed in the vehicle or with the
vehicle. Most divers will give the interior of a submerged vehicle a
cursory examination before winching it to the surface. The more experienced teams will roll the windows down if possible.

Exterior Damage

Often exterior vehicle damage is of little evidentiary value because of
the inability to determine if the damage occurred before the vehicle was

submerged, during submersion, or as a result of the salvage operation. Any damage to the undercarriage and hoses must be presumed to have resulted from the salvage operation. Even in waters of minimal visibility, there are some procedures that can be performed to minimize loss of trace evidence.

Stolen Vehicles

The most obvious indication that a vehicle has been stolen is the absence of ignition keys. Other indications of theft might include hot wires, blocked steering wheel or gas pedal, intrusion marks on doors, windows and trunk, also the absence of valuable accessories such as radio, tape decks, speakers, cellular phone, hubcaps, etc. Generally, the driver's side window will be down or driver side door unlocked to allow for someone standing outside the vehicle to accelerate the vehicle. Should the keys be in the ignition the probability of the vehicle having been stolen has been significantly reduced. A hand search of the interior of the vehicle for ignition keys can be performed in waters of limited visibility. If the vehicle has been stolen and it has been used in the commission of a crime, there may be fruits or instrumentalities of the crime that may be lost during recovery. The license plate number and the vehicle identification number, if retrievable, may allow a computer check to determine the status of the vehicle. However, all stolen vehicles are not immediately reported nor are the crimes that are committed using a stolen auto. It may prove the best policy to treat all vehicles to be recovered, unless otherwise certain, as a vehicle that may have been used in the commission of an offense.

Evidence Collection

There is a considerable amount of information that can be obtained from a submerged vehicle before efforts are made to raise it. If access into the vehicle is practicable, and can be accomplished safely, an examination of the glove compartment can be made. All items in the glove compartment should be removed and placed in plastic bags (leave water in the bags with the contents). The floors of the vehicle can be examined, photographed, and if anything is discovered, tagged and bagged. The most innocuous of items may prove to be useful. The underside of seats and behind the rear cushions should be examined and items discovered retrieved.

An exterior examination of the vehicle should be conducted similar to the preflight "walk around" conducted by pilots of small aircraft. All exterior damage should be sketched, noted, and photographed. If the vehicle has been used in a hit and run, there will be external evidence of that episode. All windows should be assessed and described. Impact bursts on the windows may have occurred as a result of an occupant striking the window or a pedestrian striking the window. Without a written or photographic record of the starburst pattern on a windshield, there will be no evidence of it after salvage since the damaged window will probably burst upon raising the vehicle.

Lights

It would be helpful to the investigation to know whether the lights were intact prior to recovery because they too are often a casualty of the salvaging operation. If the light lenses are intact prior to raising the vehicle no false assumptions will be made as to how the lenses were broken if they should be broken during the salvaging of the auto. If the lenses are not intact prior to raising the auto, a bit of evidentiary information has been obtained. If there are pieces of the lens still in place, they will probably not be in place upon recovering the vehicle. The pieces therefore, should be photographed, bagged, and tagged prior to lifting the vehicle.

The fact that the light switch is on or off is not always indicative of whether the lights were on at the time the vehicle entered the water. In salvage operations the light switch will likely be struck by debris thrown forward as the vehicle is raised by its rear axle. The light bulbs from the lights themselves can often reveal whether or not the lights were on when the vehicle entered the water. A retrieval of the light bulbs may prove to be useful as the investigation progresses.

Filaments

Burning light filaments break in a characteristic fashion upon impact that differs from filaments that break when not lighted or that simply burn out. It is important not to remove the bulbs from their housings when bulb comparisons may be necessary. Remove the entire light assembly so that damage to the bulbs and filaments will be kept at a minimum. The direction of an external impact to the front or rear of the vehicle can often be ascertained by the direction the filament is distorted.

If the vehicle has been involved in a vehicular accident or a hit and run, it will probably be subjected to a vigorous examination by the investigating officers. If there are dents, scratches, fabric, or paint on the exterior that may have been transferred by another vehicle or body, all scuba and salvage equipment will have to be eliminated before any trace evidence can be considered useful. Therefore, the salvage operation should be done with the least adverse impact upon the vehicle and all scuba and salvage equipment logged and specifically described to allow for exclusion of possible contamination by the dive and recovery team.

It should be remembered that all items packaged "wet," i.e., in a water solution, must ultimately be removed from the plastic container and dried before they can be properly examined. Items that are recovered in the water should be completely immersed in the medium from which they were retrieved, not damp because mildew will rapidly begin. Turning the items over to the lab "wet" will then leave the drying and preserving responsibility up to the laboratory technicians.

Recovery Checklist

What follows is a checklist for every submerged auto recovery operation:

a. Photos should be taken whenever possible from all cardinal directions and from above.
b. A "swim around" inventory should be done, taking in all gross features of the vehicle, including windows, doors, tires, body, and trim (all impressions from the "swim around" should be recorded).
c. A specific examination of lights and lenses should be conducted.
d. A check for intrusion marks on the body of the vehicle should be made.
e. Divers should check for license plates front and back.
f. Vehicle Identification Numbers should be recorded.
g. The vehicle should be examined for occupants.
h. Divers should check for evidence or contraband.
i. Contents of glove compartment should be bagged.
j. Sunvisors should be examined.
k. Remember that certain surfaces will retain fingerprints even in water, e.g., glass, mirrored surfaces.

Occupant recovery should always be conducted in the water. Much evidentiary information will be lost if the occupants are left in the vehicle during the recovery operation. Any postmortem injuries to the body resulting from contact with the interior of the vehicle during recovery will only complicate the autopsy.

Auto Recovery

Although most vehicle recovery is done by tow truck, floating vehicles with air bags is a method whereby nothing inside the vehicle is disturbed and exterior damage and undercarriage damage are kept to a minimum. Companies that distribute salvage equipment have pontoon bags that can be attached to the side of the vehicle with a yoke that allows the diver using a topside air compressor to inflate both pontoons simultaneously.

Water, current, bottom and vehicle conditions will dictate what type recovery technique is to be employed. Whatever method is applied, the following warnings promulgated in part by Mark Lonsdale (1989) of the Specialized Tactical Training Unit are worth remembering:

a. Do a complete site survey before diving, with special attention to strong currents and debris in the water.
b. The team leader must do a risk assessment balancing the benefit and importance of the recovery with the danger to divers.
c. Stay on the uphill side of the vehicle in case it should move or roll into deeper water.
d. Do not enter the vehicle all the way.
e. Do not enter the vehicle without a dive buddy in immediate attendance.
f. Beware of strong currents.
g. Withdraw from the vehicle during lifting of the vehicle.
h. Foresee the possibility of straps and cables not holding.
i. Know your lifting equipment and its limitations.
j. Never hurry and make decisions based on sound judgement and not favorable conjecture.
k. Do no harm. Or at least keep it to a minimum.

FIREARMS

The recovery of firearms is a straightforward proposition. No expensive lift equipment is necessary and the time involved in the recovery is minimal once the firearm has been located. The location and mapping of firearms should be handled in the same fashion as for any other important submerged evidence described in earlier chapters. The recovery method usually employed is to simply hand the weapon to someone on shore or in a boat. Why weapons are handled in such a cavalier fashion is demonstrative of a lack of appreciation of the effect of water on ferrous metals, and the potential transient evidence contained in every firearm.

Recovery Purposes

The recovery and preservation of firearms is accomplished for four purposes: medicolegal examination, ballistic comparisons, weapon identification, and in remote instances, fingerprint examination. The likelihood of discovering fingerprints on a weapon that has been submerged even for a short period of time is remote. However, there are parts of the firearm that may still render a classifiable latent. Any ammunition in the weapon may retain fingerprint impressions and should be extracted and examined for prints before preservation procedures are begun. The ammunition can be placed in a container of fresh water but handled as though fingerprints were present. The ammunition in these weapons should be considered live and the weapon loaded until rendered otherwise. Additionally, the intact bullets should be examined to determine the type of gunpowder used by the manufacturer.

Most manufacturers use flaked gunpowder, Winchester Western is the primary user of ball-shaped gunpowder. A nonjacketed bullet fired from a cartridge loaded with ball powder shows typical small indentations resembling pockmarks on its base. These are due to the explosion in the cartridge at the time of discharge, which, by increasing the pressure in the cartridge, imprints the spherical grains of gunpowder on the lead base of the bullet. If a lead bullet has been retrieved at the scene of a crime demonstrating ball powder characteristics, it would be helpful to know that the ammunition recovered from a submerged weapon was loaded with ball powder. Although not determinative ballistic evidence it is strongly suggestive evidence.

A firearm retrieved from salt water after lengthy submersion may appear relatively unaffected. Once retrieved and subjected to the air, oxidation will begin immediately and thorough rusting may progress in less than an hour rendering ballistic examination impossible. It is therefore crucial to keep the weapon immersed in water until the preservation procedure can be begun. When a firearm is properly retrieved and maintained, preservation techniques may allow ballistics tests to be conducted on the weapon and its ammunition. All firearms need to be preserved for testing and that preservation begins with the divers who recover the weapon immersing it in water.

Serial Numbers

Every firearm is stamped with a variety of numbers. The serial number is useful in determining original ownership of the weapon. Serial numbers may be more readily apparent immediately upon discovery by the dive team than later after mishandling and oxidation have occurred. One of the initial acts of the dive team should be to record and photograph the serial number in the water if visibility allows. Once rusting begins, and it happens very quickly, retrieval of the serial number may be difficult or impossible.

Serial numbers are usually stamped with hard metal dies. These dies strike the metal surface with a force that allows each digit to sink into the metal at a prescribed depth. Restoration of serial numbers can be accomplished because the metal crystals in the stamped zone are placed under a permanent strain that extends a short distance beneath the original numbers. When an etching agent is applied, the strained area will dissolve at a faster rate as compared to the underlying uncorroded metal, thus permitting the underlying number pattern to appear in the form of the original numbers. The recovery of serial numbers using etching acids is governed by the extent of corrosion of the firearm. It is therefore readily apparent that corrosion must be confined to that occurring at the time of recovery and not added to by exposing the firearm to oxidizing agents.

Barrel Blowback

In addition to fingerprint and ballistic evidence, a firearm, especially a handgun, may also contain hair, tissue, blood, and fibers. The muzzle blast of a gun fired in contact with a body and the negative pressure in the barrel following discharge may cause blood, hair, tissue fragments and fabric to be found several inches back inside the barrel (Spitz, W.U., 1993:319).

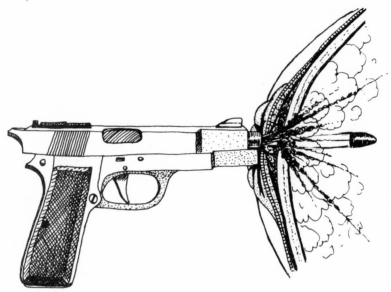

Figure 16. A weapon fired when in contact with the skull or body will have human tissue and blood as barrel residue from gas blowback.

It should be apparent that retrieving a weapon by inserting something into the barrel will only serve to dislodge and destroy any trace evidence. It is best to hold the weapon by the trigger guard or the checkered portion of the grip or stock.

The perception that a submerged firearm is rift of any relevant forensic information is erroneous. The perception that human tissue, hair, and blood will be displaced from the barrel of a firearm as a result of submersion is also erroneous. Vincent Bugliosi (1992), in his book, *And the Sea Will Tell,* described the testimony of an FBI serologist who testified during the trial of Buck Walker for the grizzly death of Mac and Muff Graham. The serologist testified that after three years submersion in the Pacific Ocean, a metal container in which it was believed that Muff Graham had been dismembered, burnt, and submerged, tested positive on a phenolphthalein screening test. The phenolphthalein screen is sensitive to a drop of blood in ten thousandths parts of water. However, this screen only determines if the sample in question is blood, not whether the blood is human. The serologist went on to describe a second test that he performed called an ouchterlony screen which does determine if a blood specimen is human. After three years of submersion, sand, water and marine intrusion the serologist was still able to determine that the cloth sample removed from the submerged case was stained with human blood (Bugliosi, V., 1992:279).

VESSELS

Boats are not usually stolen for the purpose of committing a crime and then scuttled to avoid discovery. Most boat salvage is not done for investigative purposes. A recovery team may, however, be called upon to investigate a suspected boat arson or explosion. This type of underwater operation is limited to areas of good visibility. There are no tools to provide information to the underwater arson investigator other than sight.

Arson/Detonation

For the investigator the main task is to determine if a fire or explosion was incendiary (arson) or accidental. To aid in the investigation, dive team members must have some idea of what type of incendiary evidence may be available. If the hull is intact, a visual examination can be performed aimed at locating portions of the vessel that are charred and those left unscathed. A detailed photographic log should be made describing burn characteristics and any evidence discovered. Each piece of evidence to be recovered should be photographed in its original place and condition once uncovered. The scene sketch should show the location of each piece of evidence within the search site.

Fires

Fires burn in a prescribed fashion from ignition point upward. The probable point of origin will most likely be located closest to the lowest point that shows the most intense burning characteristics. The surface of charred wood bears a pattern of crevices that is similar in appearance to the skin of an alligator. The probable point of origin is in the area where the smallest checks in the alligator pattern and the deepest charring are found. An ice pick pushed into the charred area may prove helpful in measuring depth of charring. It is in this area that the physical evidence of criminal design is most likely to be discovered. It is this point from which wood samples should be taken for laboratory examination for hydrocarbons (accelerants).

Accelerants

An examination of the charring pattern may also reveal the presence of an accelerant. Nothing should be touched or moved before measurements, sketches, and photographs have been taken.

The presence of hydrocarbon containers should be noted. In most arsons an incendiary or detonation device of some type is employed to allow the arsonist to depart the scene or to establish an alibi. Such devices may be complex remote control detonators or simply a candle bedded in gasoline. Remnants of delay devices may be discovered near the point of origin. In the case of explosions, a larger area should be searched looking for incendiary or detonation devices or their remains.

Unburned fabric may retain measurable amounts of hydrocarbons. If the interior of the boat was splashed with diesel fuel, kerosene, or gasoline, any unburned porous material may retain traces of the accelerant.

Streamers and Plants

"Streamers," also called "Plants," are flammable materials such as rags, straw, paper etc., laid to guide a fire to other areas or to spread the fire. If "streamers" were used to aid in acceleration unburned remains may be found. Cloth generally does not completely burn and if used as a "streamer," may still retain accelerant traces.

Hydrocarbons dissipate more slowly in water. It is imperative that any evidence removed from the vessel, from which hydrocarbon laboratory results are desired, be packaged in water in watertight containers. Plastic polyethylene bags are not suitable for packaging specimens because they react with hydrocarbons. Arson investigators often use clean paint cans for transporting evidence of arson.

Gas Chromatography

The gas chromatograph is the most reliable instrument for detecting flammable residues. Most arsons are initiated by petroleum distillates such as gasoline, diesel fuel, and kerosene, all of which are composed of a mixture of hydrocarbons. The gas chromatograph separates the hydrocarbons into its constituent components, giving a visual recording of the characteristic pattern of the specific petroleum product (Saferstein, 1990:290). In recovering evidence of suspected accelerants it is necessary to provide an uncontaminated control sample of the same material if available.

Ignitors

The search should include efforts to locate ignitors. The simplest ignitor is a match; however, most matches are consumed in the fire. There are many types of ignitors that might be used that could survive a fire including firearms, ammunition, "Molotov cocktail," and mechanical devices. Broken glass from a "Molotov cocktail" may contain fingerprints or reveal the type of glass container used.

EXPLOSIONS

The steps employed in the investigation of an explosion are generally the same as that for arson. There are several additional considerations. The chances of finding a large amount of trace evidence are remote. Like fire, an explosion is the product of combustion accompanied by the creation of gases and heat. It is the sudden buildup of expanding gas pressure at the point of detonation that produces the disruption of the explosion. Chemical explosions can be classified on the basis of the velocity of energy waves transmitted upon detonation.

Low order explosions involve a relatively slow rate of conversion to a gaseous state. The energy wave generated travels at a speed of less than 1,000 meters per second. The most widely used explosives in the low order group are black powder and smokeless powder. Low order explosives can be ignited by heat and are usually ignited with a lighted fuse.

High order explosives change rapidly to a gaseous state upon ignition. The energy wave created travels at a rate between 1,000 and 9,000 meters per second. Dynamite is the most commonly used high order explosive. High order explosives include dynamite or composition C-4 (made of RDX the most popular and powerful of the military explosives). Unlike low order explosives, high explosives must be detonated by an initiating device.

Initiators

The most commonly used initiator is a blasting cap. However, the ignition switch on a boat can be used to provide the spark necessary to detonate high explosives.

The search should focus on locating the site of the device and identifying the type of explosive used. The point of detonation can often be ascertained by the gaping hole left and the accompanying scorching. The type of explosive used may be determined by inspecting the residue at the scene. Wood and Fiberglas samples surrounding the detonation point should have sufficient residue to allow identification of the explosive. The entire area must be systematically searched to recover any trace of a detonating mechanism. Air lifts may be necessary to sift through the debris at the site. Particles of explosives will be embedded in the pipe cap or threads of a pipe bomb. All materials gathered from the site of an explosion must be labeled with all pertinent information. All items recovered should be packaged in separate containers.

Many manufacturers of dynamite include magnetic microtaggants in each stick of dynamite. These florescent, color-coded, multilayered particles identify the residue as dynamite and indicate the source of manufacture. The color should make the taggants visible to ultraviolet light and their magnetism susceptible to a magnet. Electric shunts from blasting caps, clock mechanisms, batteries, and pieces of wrapper may survive the explosion and concomitant fire.

In those instances where humans have been the victims of a vessel fire their remains should be bagged as described in the chapter on the investigation of deaths. The clothing should not be removed.

Insurance Companies

Insurance companies are anxious to cooperate with arson investigations, especially in those instances where the vessel is insured. The American Insurance Association in New York City has established a 24-hour Property Insurance Loss Reporting System. This is a computerized system designed to detect patterns of arson and insurance fraud nationwide. Arsonists who change geographical location or insurance companies may be apprehended with the assistance of the Property Insurance Loss Reporting System.

Boat Arson/Detonation Report

Data that should be included in the report of a suspected vessel arson/detonation:

a. General Data
   1. Owner's name.
   2. Insurer's name.
   3. Date and time of fire.
   4. Last user's name.
   5. Time and date of last use.
b. Owner Data
   1. Financial condition of owners.
   2. Prior loss history.
   3. Prior criminal history.
   4. Name of the insured.
   5. Name of the insurer.
   6. Claims history.
   7. Other boat ownership, past and present.
   8. Other insurers, past and present.
   9. Owner satisfaction with vessel.
   10. Property distribution, divorce, or partner dissolution.
c. Vessel Data
   1. Vessel condition prior to fire.
   2. Value of the property.
   3. Insured value of the property.
   4. Payment history on boat mortgage.
   5. A description of vessel furnishings will be important in the chemical analysis of evidence.
   6. Condition and location of electrical wiring prior to fire.
   7. Condition and location of diesel and gas lines prior to fire.
   8. Condition and location of propane lines to galley stoves prior to fire.
   9. Storage of flammable fluids, based on information provided by the owner.
   10. Types of fuels used.
   11. Presence of ignition keys.
d. Fire Assessment
   1. Name of the party reporting the fire.
   2. Name of party discovering fire.

3. Time interval between discovery and reporting.
4. Names of witnesses to the fire.
5. Was there a witnessed explosion?
6. Speed of travel of the fire.
7. Direction of spread of the fire.
8. Location of the vessel when fire was reported?

e. Fire Investigation
 1. Search site.
 2. Recovery site.
 3. Point of origin of the fire.
 4. Was there evidence of accelerants?
 5. Was there evidence of incendiary devices?
 6. Was there evidence of explosive devices?
 7. Was there evidence of ignitors/detonators?
 8. Describe burn characteristics.
 9. List recovered evidence, their location and how they are packaged.
10. Valuable items missing, i.e., telemetry systems, television, stereo, speakers, backup engine, dinghy.
11. Insured's explanation of the fire should be consistent with an examination of the remains specifically as to cause of fire, point of origin, type of smoke, speed and direction of spread.

The ultimate objective of every search and investigation is to uncover evidence that may ultimately assist in resolving questions pertaining to the investigation. Often special evidence technicians are available to assist in evidence collection in land investigations. Evidence technicians, arson investigators, explosive specialists, forensic scientists, criminalists, and forensic investigators have yet to get their feet wet. It is, therefore, incumbent upon the underwater recovery diver to be aware of the possible site of potential evidence so as to preserve such evidence for laboratory examination.

REFERENCES

Bugliosi, V. 1992. *And The Sea Will Tell.* New York: Ivy Books.
Lonsdale, M.V. 1989. *SRT Diver.* Los Angeles: Author.
Miller, L.S. and Brown, A.M. 1990. *Criminal Evidence Laboratory Manual.* Cincinnati: Anderson.

O'hara, C.E. and O'Hara, G.L. 1988. *Fundamentals of Criminal Investigation,* 5th ed., Springfield: Charles C Thomas.

Saferstein, R. 1990. *Criminalistics: An Introduction to Forensic Science.* Englewood Cliffs: Prentice Hall.

Spitz, W.U. 1993. *Medicolegal Investigation of Death,* 3rd ed. Springfield: Charles C Thomas.

Stoffel, J.F. 1972. *Explosives and Homemade Bombs.* Springfield: Charles C Thomas.

Yinton, J., and Zitrin, S. 1981. *The Analysis of Explosives.* Oxford: Pergamon Press.

Chapter 9

MEDICOLEGAL ASPECTS OF UNDERWATER DEATH

The history of public service diving has been one of fire departments providing water rescue services to the community. As part of that responsibility, fire departments have provided water rescue, search, and body recovery operations. The prevailing presumption has been that if a body is found in the water or reported as having drowned, the precipitating event was accidental. Police agencies have historically referred calls about drowning victims to fire departments, lending credence to the notion that a death underwater was accidental until proven otherwise. The fallacy of this perspective has been the historic destruction or contamination of transient and trace evidence in the recovery process that may have provided information upon which the determination of death as a homicide could have been made. Police agencies and fire departments should treat sudden death under any circumstances as a possible homicide until investigation establishes the cause and mechanism of death. This approach undoubtedly will increase the workload of an already overburdened dive recovery team. The alternative is to lose evidence of a homicide based on a universally held and occasionally erroneous presumption.

Once a body has been located and measurements recorded, it must be raised to the surface. It is during the recovery portion of the operation that evidence can be preserved or irredeemably destroyed or contaminated.

All bodies should be bagged in the water. There will always be those cases where rigor and putrefaction make underwater bagging difficult, but a failure to bag in the water may result in the loss of transient evidence, such as hair or fiber, and the destruction or contamination of trace evidence, such as accelerant residue. Hands should be bagged in plastic bags with wrist pull ties to preserve any tissue, broken fingernails, fiber, or gunpowder that may be retrieved from the hands and fingers. Feet and shoes should be bagged in plastic bags with ankle pull ties to preserve any trace evidence in the shoe soles and to compare wear patterns of footwear. The head should be bagged in a plastic bag with neck pull ties to alert the recovery team to any injuries to the head that occur during recovery. All bags should be firmly placed with consideration for any possible premortem ligature marks. All evidence recovered from water should be accompanied by a sample of the bottom structure as a control for laboratory analysis.

A body recovered from an Austin, Texas lake with a serious laceration to the scalp was believed to have been the victim of a homicide. Upon raising the body to the surface unbagged, and placing it on the recovery vessel, fire fighters noted a large deep gash on the scalp. The police were notified and an investigation begun. A subsequent examination by the medical examiner determined that the wound to the scalp was postmortem and most likely the result of an impact with the recovery vessel's propellers. The investigation was called off; the media was not.

A number of criticisms might be made of that recovery. However, the main point is that, if the head had been bagged and if the death had been treated as part of a homicide investigation, the head wound would not have occurred or if it had, it would have been evident that the head wound was inflicted postmortem and the subsequent embarrassment avoided.

IDENTIFICATION

An investigation of unattended deaths may focus on questions of identity. Whether accidental death or homicide, the identity of an unknown decedent is important. Identification begins where and when the body is found and proceeds backward, gravitating to the individuals and places the unidentified person contacted prior to death. Evidence at the scene of where the deceased was going or had been are the pathways leading to identification. Most unidentified dead are violent deaths and the inability to identify the body serves as an obstacle to further investigation and the trail grows cold.

Identification methods may be described as primary or secondary. Primary identifications would include friend, relative, and next of kin; dental comparisons, radiographic comparison of prior injuries and surgeries; and classifiable fingerprints. Secondary methods include all other identifiers that enable a comparison to confirm or exclude identity. Secondary methods would include jewelry, eye glasses, birthmarks, congenital abnormalities, tattoos, scars, race, color of hair, blood type, sex, age. The key to identification is to discover features in an unidentified person that compare to the same documented features in a missing person.

Personal Effects

Personal effects, clothing, and gross anatomical features are the first items available for examination in attempting to determine identification. In mass disasters, descriptions of clothing and personal effects are provided by next of kin. Billfolds contain drivers licenses, credit cards, and personal papers. Jewelry is often unique and engraved. Keys are often distinctive in design and function, characterizing them as door keys, auto keys, brief case keys, suitcase keys, and a successful unlocking provides a tentative identification.

The decomposed body of a man washed ashore at a beach resort area. An unusual key bearing the letter K was found in his jeans' pocket. A review of local missing persons did not reveal an identity. Ship movements in and out of the harbor for several weeks prior to his appearance were investigated and the ships contacted for any missing crewmen. One ship was missing a cook who disappeared during a storm at sea. The key in the dead man's pocket fit the ship's refrigerator door (Fiero, M.F. 1993:85).

Teeth

Teeth are resistant to decomposition and, therefore, are a common method of positive identification. The major problem associated with teeth is the care that must be given them during the recovery procedure and to assure that all teeth in and around skeletonized remains have been found. A person's occupation or oral habits may impact upon the teeth. Carpenters and electricians who grip nails between their teeth may have notched upper incisors. Tailors may have similar smaller notches. Musicians who play wind instruments often clench the mouthpiece between their teeth leaving broad worn areas on the upper teeth. Long-time pipe smokers may have developed a diamond-shaped gap between upper and lower clenched teeth. Nicotine stains will be found on the surfaces of the teeth of heavy pipe and cigarette smokers. The presence of poor oral hygiene, many decayed teeth, and swollen gums are usually indicative of low economic status.

Feet

The shod foot survives burning, decomposition, marine animal depredation and water damage more consistently than do hands and especially fingers. The investigator's focus is generally on hands, finger and palm prints. Soft unprotected tissues are the first site of marine animal depredation and least likely to render discernable, classifiable characteristics. Feet and the shoes they bear may provide readily available identification information. Wear patterns of footwear's outer and inner soles are sufficiently unique to permit comparisons for exclusionary purposes.

POSTMORTEM CHANGES

After death physicochemical changes occur which lead to the dissolution of all soft tissues. The importance of these changes is in their sequential nature, which can be used in arriving at an approximate time of death. Knowledge of these changes can also alert us to the destructive changes brought about by decomposition thereby avoiding confusing these changes for premortem injuries.

Using postmortem changes as a timing mechanism is generally based in part on the physicochemical changes evident upon examination of the body, such as rigor mortis and putrefaction (decomposition).

Rigor Mortis

Following death, muscles become flaccid, followed by a stiffness which freezes the joints and is known as rigor mortis. In temperate climates rigor becomes apparent within an hour and progresses for twelve hours. After maximum rigor has set in, usually during a twelve-hour period, the rigor begins to progressively disappear during the following twelve hours. Rigor mortis develops at a similar rate in all muscles. Smaller muscles become involved in rigor more quickly than larger muscles, giving rise to the misbelief that rigor progresses from the head down.

The progression of rigor may be substantially modified by a variety of factors which affect the underlying chemical process. The appearance and disappearance of rigor may be slowed by cold. Rigor is also affected by total body muscle mass and develops poorly in young children, the elderly, and the debilitated. The variability of postmortem rigor makes it unreliable as an index as to the time of death and only has value when used with other timing devices.

PUTREFACTION

Putrefaction is one of death's realities that recovery divers must contend with. Attempting to raise a decomposing body by attaching lines or towing by an arm or leg will prove less than satisfactory. Decomposing bodies must be bagged in the water, the alternative is to retrieve it in bits and pieces.

Rigor Mortis of the involuntary muscles and putrefaction are often viewed as indices of time of death. The rate of putrefaction depends on the physical environment in which the body reposes. It is generally accepted that putrefaction in air is more rapid than in water, which is more rapid than in soil. One week in air equals two weeks in water and eight weeks in soil (Perper, J.A. 1993:32). Putrefaction of a submerged body proceeds at a slower rate than does putrefaction of a body on land. Once the body has been removed from the water, putrefaction will accelerate. Putrefaction in seawater is slower than in fresh water because the salt retards the growth of bacteria. In stagnant waters, bacteria usually abound and decomposition is swift.

Water temperature will also affect that rate of decomposition. As water depths increase water temperatures can be expected to decrease and the rate of decomposition will slow. In evaluating postmortem changes it is important to consider outside temperature, temperature at the water's surface and the temperature at the depth from which the body is recovered.

In temperate climates, decomposition on the surface begins within 24 to 30 hours. In water, decomposition will generally begin within 48 to 60 hours. Putrefaction generally begins as a greenish discoloration of the right lower abdomen followed by a gaseous bloating and a purple discoloration of the face and bulging of the eyes. The tongue protrudes from the mouth and decomposition fluids are purged from the nose and mouth.

Discoloration spreads within 72 to 96 hours to the chest, arms, and legs. Discoloration of the skin may have progressed sufficiently and become so dark as to mistake white individuals for blacks. Immersion and putrefaction both cause the skin to slip. The skin of the hands, legs, and feet may shed in a glovelike and stocking-like fashion. The shed skin can still be processed for finger printing to help identify the deceased.

Once the body has completely decomposed and has fully skeletonized, the bones may last for centuries. Bones that have been immersed for long periods may demineralize and turn to dust upon touching. Handling skeletonized remains should be kept at a minimum.

Ocular Changes

Eyes may exhibit the earliest postmortem changes. A thin corneal film may begin to develop within minutes of death. Corneal cloudiness develops within three hours of death. If the eyes are closed the appearance of corneal filming and clouding may be delayed for 24 hours or longer.

Postmortem Lividity

Once the heart no longer circulates blood through the body, gravity causes blood to pool in the lower parts of the body. This pooling blood imparts a purple color to the lower body parts and a paleness to the upper body. Lividity is most apparent in bodies that have lain on land. Blood pooling can often indicate that the body discovered on land has been moved after death. If the body is placed in a position other than the position of death an absence of lividity in the lower portions suggests the body has been moved. Bodies in water should show little evidence of lividity because of the water's buoyancy. Should lividity be prominent, death prior to submersion should be suspected.

COMMON ERRORS IN INTERPRETING CHANGES

Often postmortem changes may be misinterpreted making identification of the deceased difficult sending investigators down a dead end. The following is a partial list of misinterpretations that may be made as a result of postmortem changes:

1. Postmortem bloating of the body may create an appearance of obesity.
2. Purged fluid may be mistaken for blood caused by an antemortem trauma.

3. Postmortem dilatation and flaccidity of the vagina and anus may produce the appearance of a sexual attack.
4. The diffusion of blood into tissues may be difficult to distinguish from antemortem bruising.
5. Skin shedding may be seen as an antemortem thermal injury.
6. Skin discoloration may cause erroneous racial classification.

The problems in relying upon the results of rigor mortis and putrefaction in determining time of death are the variation in the environment and individual characteristics which impact on the determination of time of death. The metabolic state of the individual plays a significant role in postmortem changes as does the environmental characteristics in which the postmortem changes occur. Time of death, therefore, can only be broadly estimated within a variable time frame. The longer the time between death and discovery, the less effective are time of death estimates and the wider the range of the time variable. Keeping in mind the shortcomings inherent in estimating time of death, the following approach is generally applied:

1. An initial determination of a wide "window of death" is established and subsequently narrowed as additional information becomes available. The "window of death" is defined as the time interval from positive ascertainment of life to time of discovery of the remains. The "window of death" should be established according to the most reliable testimony or evidence as to when the individual was last alive.

2. Using individual postmortem changes, taking into consideration temperature and physical characteristics of the deceased, a conservative time of death range can be established.

DROWNING

Drowning is mostly accidental. In some instances drowning may be suicidal. Police investigators are often confronted with a body that has been placed in the water for purposes of disposal. It is the differences between drowning and postmortem immersion that are the focal point for the investigator. Several phases are recognized in drowning:

1. Breath holding lasts until accumulating carbon dioxide in the blood and tissues causes stimulation of the respiratory center in the brain and inhalation of water.

2. Swallowing of water, coughing, vomiting and rapid loss of consciousness.
3. Convulsions associated with gasping precede respiratory arrest, which is followed by failure of the heart, brain damage, and death.

The central question in body recovery from waterways is whether the individual was alive at the time of submersion. The scene surrounding the drowning and the deceased's clothing may provide information as to how the body came to be in the water.

A young man was found in shallow water. A short distance from the body was found an empty bottle of wine. The wine bottle cap was screwed in place. Upon examination of the deceased it was noted that his pants zipper was open. The initial impression was that the young man was intoxicated and fell into the water while urinating. Subsequent autopsy findings confirmed that he had a blood alcohol of 0.21. Lack of turbulence of the water in which the man was found suggested that water in the stomach was from drowning as opposed to turbulent water action. An examination of the crime scene and the deceased's clothing strongly suggested drowning as opposed to foul play. The investigators theory was borne out by the autopsy results. Often the environment surrounding the drowning and the clothing of the deceased will reveal as much as a subsequent autopsy.

Exudate

Abundant foam can be found exuding from the mouth and nostrils of most drowning victims. An attempt at resuscitation may apply sufficient pressure on the chest to cause the exudate to become visible. The foam is a mixture of mucus, air, and water. The presence of this mixture in the airway suggests that the victim was alive at the time of submersion. As decomposition progresses the fluid turns a foul-smelling brown.

The significance of bloodstained foam in the respiratory passages of a body recovered from water was an important issue at a 1969 court hearing in Wilkes-Barre, Pennsylvania, regarding the death of Mary Jo Kopechne. At this hearing, arguments were heard regarding whether or not Kopechne's body should be exhumed for autopsy to determine the cause of death.

The judge refused to order an exhumation based on the testimony that a large amount of pinkish foam exuded from her nose and mouth after she was recovered from the water. This finding led to the conclusion that Miss Kopechne had to be alive, and therefore drowned, when the car in which she was a passenger drove off a bridge at Chappaquiddick Island, off the Massachusetts Coast (Spitz, W.U. 1993:502).

Skin

Skin wrinkling of the hands and feet is frequently referred to as washerwoman's skin. Contrary to certain misconceptions, washerwoman's skin has nothing to do with drowning but is a product of immersion. Skin wrinkling can begin as early as thirty minutes in water of 50 degrees.

Gloving begins in warm waters within several hours while in cold waters may not begin for several days. When the skin sheds from the hands and feet the finger and toenails are shed also. The shed skin may be inked to obtain finger and sole prints for the purposes of identification. Both the inner and outer surfaces of shed skin will render a print.

Flotation

A body in fresh water sinks to the bottom unless air is trapped in the clothing. In salt water a body may float several feet below the surface and be visible to low flying search aircraft. In either case the body may completely surface when tissue gas has formed as a result of putrefaction. Gas formation generally begins in the gastrointestinal tract. The time of the reappearance of the body depends on water temperature, and ante-mortem diet. Gases formed are easily compressed; in cold deep waters gas formation may be suppressed or not occur at all. There are a number of commercial products available that allow the charting of water temperature that theoretically produce a refloatation time. The variables in postmortem gas formation are such that any estimate of refloatation time based on any theory is strictly guesswork.

River Current

In waters with currents in excess of three miles per hour, lividity is more a product of current direction than of gravity. The parts of the body facing downstream may develop the purple color characteristic of lividity with the part of the body facing upstream concomitantly pale. It should be noted that rivers with currents in excess of three knots are not suitable for diver recovery. River currents in excess of three knots have proven unnecessarily hazardous to divers.

River currents may move the body across the bottom. The drowning victim is often found in a head down fetal position. Abrasions can be found on the forehead, forearms, knees, knuckles, nose, and toes as a result of being drug by the current. These abrasions may be misinterpreted as evidence of postmortem trauma or as defense wounds.

Marine Depredation

Marine life feed on the soft part of the victim's face. Often postmortem injuries to the eyelids, lips, nose, and ears are mistaken for traumatic antemortem injuries. A variety of algae may cover the exposed parts of the body giving a green or black hue to those areas. A body may be so covered with algae as to give the impression the body is covered in mud and makes identification and time of death determination more difficult.

In April, 1976, a body of a woman without head or hands was found floating in an upstate New York lake. She had a peculiar gash under the left breast. The corpse was covered with green algae. The medical examiner, who was a hospital pathologist, determined that the slim, athletic body belonged to a woman in her late twenties and that she had been dead for three weeks. Broadcasts on television and radio brought no response to the identity of the decapitated woman. Dr. Michael Baden, Chief Medical Examiner for the City of New York, examined the body and determined that the woman's age was closer to fifty-five and that there had been an identifiable scar or tattoo removed from under the breast to prevent identification. Dr. Baden sent samples of the algae to a biologist who examined the algae and discovered two generations of algae. Fresh green algae had formed during the recent year and dead algae was present from a prior year, concluding that the woman had been dead for at least a year and a half. Following the public announcement of the new age, time of death, and possible identifying scar, the body was promptly identified by the woman's sister, who suspected that her brother-in-law had killed his wife.

Vehicular Drownings

It may be thought that individuals who drive their vehicles into the water and drown should bear some evidence of the trauma experienced when the vehicle strikes the water. Autopsies of such victims consistently find no evidence of injury. Even in vehicles plummeting 100 feet to the water the occupants usually bear no evidence of impact. It appears that the water sufficiently cushions the impact to prevent traumatic injuries.

THERMAL INJURIES

Vessel and aircraft fires and explosions often leave the underwater recovery team with bodies and debris that have been burned and that require specific procedures in recovery and investigation. Vessel and aircraft explosions may result in fires. Aircraft crashes are often accompanied by fire. Whether the fires and explosion are the product of accident, negligence, or criminal enterprise the investigation will focus on the underwater recovery site and the evidence obtained therefrom. Underwater investigators may mistake seriously burned bodies recovered from underwater as displaying signs of advanced putrefaction.

Approximately 70 percent of the human body is composed of water and 25 percent is combustible organic tissue. The remaining 5 percent is noncombustible inorganic compounds, primarily salts and calcium phosphate. Vessel fires may attain temperatures high enough to burn soft tissues but aircraft fires prior to crash and submersion are not likely to burn long enough to produce that degree of burn. Burn injury severity is directly related to the heat and duration of exposure. Most household, aircraft, or shipboard fires seldom exceed temperatures of 1300 degrees Fahrenheit. At that temperature, an adult body will not burn completely.

Fire is not an effective way of disposing of a body. A crematorium must fire its chambers to 1500 degrees Fahrenheit for one and a half hours to reduce an adult body to manageable proportions. Even after that length of exposure, some large bone fragments remain and must be reduced in size before placed in a funerary vessel.

It may be possible to determine the duration of the exposure to heat of a burned body. It takes considerable time and temperature for a fire to expose the body's bones. At 1200 degrees Fahrenheit the rib cage and facial bones are exposed simultaneously in approximately 20 minutes. Shin bones are not exposed until after 25 minutes and thigh and shin bones not completely exposed until after 35 minutes (Richards, N.F. 1977). Using Richard's timetable, it may be possible to reconstruct where a vessel or aircraft fire has burned the longest, where it began, if the fire was a product of an explosion and if accelerants were used.

The use of a flammable liquid for disposal of a body results in patchy disproportionate burning. If a body recovered from an underwater repository had the face charred and the teeth destroyed while the remainder of the body is less burned, it may represent an attempt to obliterate identity prior to disposal. Chemical analysis of clothing may reveal the presence of residual accelerants. Such accelerants may still be discernable after lengthy submersion. Dried burned uncharred skin may also reveal traces of hydrocarbons.

Teeth are highly resistant to fire. If facial soft tissues are not destroyed, the lips and the mouth may be sealed by the heat and dryness thereby providing additional protection to the teeth. Recovery of bodies from aircraft or vessels that have been burned should include bottom samples as a control specimen. If the remains of clothing bear traces of hydrocarbons bottom samples will prove helpful in eliminating background contamination as a possible source.

Identification of the Burn Victim

The rate of decomposition of a burned body will be decreased significantly, just as cooked meat decomposes more slowly than does uncooked meat, thereby rendering time of death determinations based on underwater decomposition inapplicable. Absence of uniformity in decomposition suggests that decomposition was caused by heat rather than time. The rigidity of a burned body found in a pugilistic position may be mistaken for rigor mortis; this rigidity is caused by a denaturation of muscle proteins and body fluids.

Investigation of recovered burn victims should focus on two points:

1. identification, and
2. cause of death.

The usual parameters available for identification are significantly altered or no longer available in burn victims. The weight loss of a burned victim may approach 60 percent. The length of the body may be shortened by inches. Facial features are changed because of skin tightening. Fingers and hands may shrink to one-third their original size. The skin on the hands may detach as in drowning victims forming a glove, the glove includes the fingernails. The glove and the underlying skin are still subject to fingerprinting. These gloves are more fragile than those retained from the drowning victim and must be handled with care. Hair color may change, except that black hair remains black. Scars, birthmarks, moles, and tattoos may be obliterated or destroyed.

Racial identification may be impossible because of the charring unless tight clothing or shoes kept the skin intact. Intact skin is most likely to be found under belts, brassieres or shoes and in the armpits. Intact skin at the wrists or ankles may have been a product of bindings and unburned skin at the neck may be indicative of ligature strangulation.

It is difficult to distinguish a skull fracture caused by heat from one caused by trauma. Cranial fractures seen in burn victims are usually above the temple on either side. The presence of such fractures does not necessarily suggest criminal enterprise.

Just as the skull may fracture as a result of heat so may the skin split on occasion exposing the abdominal cavity. In distinguishing skin splitting because of heat from antemortem cuts and slashes it is well to note the direction and depth of the splits. Splits caused by heat only involve the skin not the underlying tissue. Heat caused splits run parallel to the muscle. Splits across a muscle are not heat related.

As a result of the shrinkage of anal tissue or as the result of abdominal gas build up, the rectal wall may protrude through the anal opening. This protrusion could be mistaken for a premortem sexual assault.

Death From Explosions

The main investigatory objectives of death caused by explosion is to: (a) identify the deceased(s), (b) reconstruct the events, (c) identify the explosive mechanism.

Identification of the decedent progresses as in any other death investigation except that body parts may be widely dispersed. Facial destruction requires that emphasis be placed on other means of identification. Fingers, feet, teeth, and dentures are the tools of identification in deaths where body parts are dispersed or intermingled.

Reconstruction of the events is dependent upon the location and extent of damage to the vessel, aircraft, or vehicle as well as the location and extent of injuries to the deceased.

In a case involving an explosion in an automobile, on-the-scene examination by investigators determined that the explosive was not in the glove compartment or affixed to the undercarriage of the vehicle. The combined investigation by the police and the medical examiner determined:

a. which of the two occupants was the driver and which the passenger;
b. that the bomb was located on the floorboard between the passenger's feet;
c. that the passenger was holding and leaning over the bomb when it exploded; and
d. that the bomb was being transported when it accidentally exploded (Spitz, W.U.; Sopher, I.M. and DiMaio, V.J.M. 1970).

Attempts to ascertain the materials of which a bomb is made is valuable in determining the identity of the perpetrator. Bomb fragments may be trapped in the clothing and body tissues of the bombing victim(s). In the auto bombing referred to above, X-rays of the passengers revealed a 1.5 volt mercury battery, a portion of a spring, several rivets and two thin metal wires buried in the body parts of the deceased. Some of the materials removed at autopsy were identified as part of a clock mechanism that was traceable to the manufacturer.

Clothing and personal effects must be treated as repositories for traces of the explosives used in the explosive device. Those victims closest to the epicenter of an explosion may have all their loose clothing blown off. In some instances death may result from massive lung hemorrhages with little or no external evidence of trauma.

MASS DISASTER

Manmade mass disasters are those in which human factors are involved. The most frequent manmade disaster is an aircraft crash. It is to this disaster that dive recovery skills may be called. Aircraft crashes are most visible because of the high profile accorded them by the media, the great number of airports, the numerous aircraft, and the potential for large numbers of injured and dead. There are an estimated two thousand aviation fatalities a year. In every aircraft crash, local authorities will be first on the scene and their conduct will often determine the success or failure of the accident investigation and play an important role in the successful identification of the dead.

As in explosions, the primary objectives are to recover the bodies, identify the bodies, and reconstruct the events. The objective of the first responding team is to secure the scene from any and all trespass. With any exterior crime scene, and aircrashes in water are no exception, it is helpful to establish three separate zones of security, each emanating from the scene center. The closest zone should not be penetrated by anyone other than forensic specialists with specific authorization and a ledger should be kept as to who enters, time of entry, time of departure and a list of what has been removed from the scene. The second tier of security should prevent anyone not actively involved in the investigation from entry. The third tier and furthest from the center of the scene should establish a perimeter that allows monitoring of all traffic approaching the crime scene from any direction. The opportunity for looting is most apparent in a mass disaster. A mass disaster plan should be developed including procedures for underwater recovery operations, for every community and every department. Specific individuals should be given responsibility and authority to keep all unauthorized personnel, including unauthorized police personnel, away from the crash site.

On June 24, 1975 Eastern Airlines flight 66 crashed in New York. Police on the scene gave each body a consecutive number, removed all valuables from the bodies and put all recovered jewelry and wallets into manilla envelopes. The envelopes were then sent to the property room to prevent theft. The bodies were lined up on the tarmac and covered with sheets. All this was done before any efforts were made to use wallet contents, jewelry, or position of the body to identify the victims. An examination of the personal property envelopes that supposedly contained the valuables and personal effects of the passengers revealed an aircraft load of paupers (Baden, M.M. 1992:84). All valuables had been removed and lost in the handling.

Although gathering and inventorying personal effects are important, it is more important not to remove any of these materials until the entire wreck site has been searched and photographed and all remains have been photographed in relationship to debris and personal effects. Most underwater investigators use 35 mm cameras and color film. Video footage often reveals a perspective that may be lost in still photography. The entire underwater site should be shot in overlaying strips and later overdubbed with narrative and then relegated to conventional 35 mm still shots.

Recovery and identification of the passengers is generally the most time-consuming part of an air crash investigation, more so if that investigation is taking place underwater. Identification can be positive or presumptive. Positive identification is based on pre and postmortem comparisons of dental records, fingerprints, palm prints, foot prints, or DNA profiling. A positive identification removes any doubt from the identification of the body. Presumptive identifications are other means of identification that result in an identification that is less than certain. Presumptive identifications require several points of inconclusive comparisons that cumulatively establish legal identity of the body.

The easiest way to begin the underwater aircrash investigation is to obtain a passenger list and seating assignment. The investigation is often hampered by bodies being torn asunder, disfigured, or mutilated as a result of impact or deceleration.

Body parts and personal possessions may be proximate to an assigned seat giving some clue as to identity. It may take time to obtain information necessary to begin identification such as flight manifest, seating assignments, family members, employers, medical and dental records.

In most cases positive identifications are made on the basis of dental comparisons. Few people today have not had dental work done on their teeth. That dental work is as individual as fingerprints.

Fingerprints are the next most common method of identification. It has been estimated that only 25 percent of the American population has fingerprints on file. Only a single fingerprint is necessary to confirm identification when compared with the fingerprint records of passengers.

In those cases involving extensive body fragmentation identification becomes more difficult. For presumptive purposes a single finger, foot, part of a dental prosthesis, eye glasses, or jaw can identify a passenger as having died in the crash. There are 209 bones in the body, any one of them may have specific characteristics that will allow identification when compared to premortem X-rays. Such an identification will allow a death certificate to be issued. An unidentified individual hampers the investigation and places the burden of an unsettled estate upon the beneficiaries.

In all crashes, the specter of a manmade explosion hovers. All clothing, personnel effects, and body parts should be handled in the same fashion as for a known bombing. Any underwater searches should include detonator components. Aircraft parts should be recovered and documented as any other evidence. The presumption in an aircraft investigation should be that criminal intervention was involved. Even those crashes where there is confirmation of accidental causes those causes will be best discovered and corroborated by treating the recovery operation as a criminal investigation.

With an air crash, investigators are subject to pressures to move quickly to determine cause and to forestall the clamor of relatives trying to determine if their loved ones were passengers. Those pressures should not affect the quality of the investigation. Underwater recovery will be a time-consuming operation and the public, media, and federal agencies must learn to accept that. This recovery operation is in every sense of the word an underwater archaeological excavation, bringing into play the panoply of underwater skills used in recovering, measuring, and processing evidence. Time, diligence, and patience are the commodities of an underwater excavation, the very same commodities are anathema to the public and the media. Once human remains have been recovered there is little reason to hurry an investigation of an air crash.

Prior use of salvage techniques rather than meticulous excavation have allowed rapid recovery of underwater evidence. The public now expects that this rapidity be employed in any such disaster. It is necessary to reeducate the public to accept a full and complete archaeological recovery operation including the additional time such an operation requires. Public relations in this type of a situation requires a masterful touch, but the investigation should involve a complete archaeological examination and excavation of the scene to assure that no evidence of identification and causation (criminal endeavor) is overlooked. Although a good working relationship with the press is desirable, it is best for recovery team members to leave such relationships to persons designated for that purpose. In dealing with the press, the following may prove helpful:

a. Keep the search scene secure and organized, anticipating covert photography.

b. All briefings and debriefings of dive team members should be done in private.

c. Recovery team members should arrive at the site together rather than to straggle in individually, casting about aimlessly.

d. Conduct and conversation should reflect the gravity of the situation at all times.

e. The release of information pertaining to victims is the province of authorized personnel only.

f. All statements to the media should be prepared statements and read to media representatives (copies of such statements should be kept as part of the file).

REFERENCES

Bass, W. M. 1987. *Human Osteology, A Laboratory and Field Manual,* 3rd ed. Columbia, MO, Missouri Archaeological Society.

Bray, M., Luke, J.L., and Blackbourne, B.D. Vitreous humor chemistry in deaths associated with rapid chilling and prolonged freshwater immersion. *J Forensic Sci, 28:*599–593, 1983.

Bray, M. Chemical estimation of fresh water immersion intervals. *Am J Forensic Med Path.* 6133–139, 1985.

Bray, M. The eye as a chemical indicator of environmental temperature at the time of death. *J Forensic Sci, 29:*389–395, 1984.

Davis, J.H. Bodies found in the water. *Am J Forensic Med Path, 78:*291–297, 1986.

DiMaio, D.J., and DiMaio, V.J.M.: Airplane Crashes. *In Forensic Pathology.* New York: Elsevier, 2989, pp. 285–288.

Fierro, M.F. Identification of Human Remains. In Spitz, W.U. 1993. *Medicolegal Investigation of Death,* 3rd ed. Springfield: Charles C Thomas.

Fisher, R.S., Spitz, W.U., Breitenecker, R. and Adams, J.E. Techniques of identification applied to 81 extremely fragmented aircraft fatalities. *J Forensic Sci, 10:*121, 1965.

Giertsen, J.C., and Morild, I. Seafaring bodies. *Am J Forensic Med Path, 10*(1):25–27, 1989.

Henahan, J.F. Fire. *Science, 80, vol. 1,* 2:29–38, 1980.

Jungbluth, W.O. Inner sole footwear comparison. *Identification News,* pp. 5–13, May 1986.

Luntz, L.L. Dental radiography and photography in identification. *Dent Radiogr Photogr, 40:*83, 1967.

McCormick, M.M. The National Transportation Safety Board and the investigation of civil aviation and transportation accidents. *Am J Forensic Med Pathol, 1:*239–243, 1980.

Perper, J.S. Time of Death and Changes After Death. In Spitz, W.U. 1993. *Medicolegal Investigation of Death,* 3rd. Springfield: Charles C Thomas.

Richards, N.F. Fire investigation-destruction of corpses. *Med Sci Law, 17:*79, 1977.

Rivers, R.W. 1980. *Traffic Accident Investigators' Handbook.* Springfield: Charles C Thomas.

Rosenbluth, E.D. A legal identification. *Dent Cosmos, 44:*1029, 1902.

Simson, L.R. Aircraft Death Investigation. A Comprehensive Review. In Curran, A.L., McGarry and Petty, C.S. (Eds) *Modern Legal Medicine, Psychiatry and Forensic Science.* Philadelphia: Davis, 1980, pp. 339–361.

Smerecki, C.J., and Lovejoy, C.O. Identification via pedal morphology. *Identification News,* pp. 3–5, 15, May 1986.

Spitz, W.U. Drowning. *Hosp Med, 5:*8, 1969.

Spitz, W.U. 1993. Drowning. *Medicolegal Investigation of Death,* 3rd ed. Springfield: Charles C Thomas.

Spitz, W.U., Sopher, I.J., and DiMaio, V.J.M. Medicolegal investigation of a bomb explosion in an automobile. *J Forensic Sci, 15:*537, 1970.

Stahl, III, C.J. Identification of Human Remains. In Spitz, W.U. and Fisher, R.S. (Eds.) *Medicolegal Investigation of Death,* 2nd ed. Springfield: Charles C Thomas.

U.S. Naval Flight Surgeon Aircraft Mishap Investigation, Pocket Reference, 2nd edition. Norfolk, Aeromedical Division, Naval Safety Center, 1989.

Teather, R.G. 1983. *The Underwater Investigator.* Fort Collins: Concept Systems, Inc.

Wagner, G.L. and Froede, R.C. *Medicolegal investigation of mass disasters.* In Spitz, W.U. Medicolegal Investigation of Death, 3rd ed. Springfield: Charles C Thomas.

Warfel, G.H. 1979. *Identification Technologies.* Springfield: Charles C Thomas.

Chapter 10

USING RECOVERED EVIDENCE
IN THE COURTROOM

An investigator who intends to participate in the satisfaction of successful prosecutions must excel at two things: documentation and
testifying. It serves no purpose for the best of investigators to take the
witness stand without adequate documentation in support of the investigation. Trials often occur months, if not years, after the investigation has
been completed. The only reliable record of the investigation is the
documentation prepared by the investigator. If that documentation is
sparse, inaccurate, or lacking basic composition skills, the testifying
investigator is at risk in attempting to remedy those shortcomings on the
witness stand.

The usual catastrophe begins by the officer testifying to facts not
included in the documentation. Such testimony is a gift to the defense. If
the testimony is important enough to tell the jury, then why was it not
included in the original report? The inference obviously is, it would
have been had it happened.

A failing memory that recovers in time for trial is also risky. If the
report was made close in time to the recovery operation would not the
documentation be a more accurate rendition of the facts than an uncor-
roborated recollection months or years later? Obviously, a contempora-
neous recording of significant events is more reliable than a recollection
months or years later and any suggestion otherwise is viewed as suspect.

Good trial lawyers are not born, they learn. Competent police witnesses are not born, they too are a product of (a) potential, (b) training,
(c) experience and (d) preparation. A superb, unprepared trial lawyer
will lose to an average prepared trial lawyer. Every time. That adage is
applicable to any witness who enters the gladiatorial arena of the law.

Preparation is reflected in the quality of the testimony. The quality of
preparation is based upon the quality of the documentation that has
been completed by the investigating officers, the time spent in studying

that documentation, and the sources from which that documentation stems.

A policeman who testifies well will assist the prosecutor in obtaining guilty verdicts. A policeman who can reliably testify will be seen by the prosecutor as an asset to cultivate. If the prosecutor accepts cases from an officer she has learned to have confidence in, that officer's conviction rate will soar. A sustained rate of convictions for any police officer cannot hurt career perspectives.

A testifying police investigator can be a defense lawyer's ally or worst nightmare. In selecting the jury, defense lawyers inquire into the venireperson's (prospective jurors) occupational background. Anyone with police relatives or police friends will most likely be struck from a jury. These prospective jurors will be asked if they believe that a police officer is any more believable than any other witness. They will be asked if they are of the opinion that police officers do not make mistakes. They will be asked if they are of the opinion that police officers do not lie. Anyone answering these questions favorably will be subjected to being peremptorily (without reason) struck.

Why does the defense counsel place so much emphasis on the police officer? He knows that the entire case may rest on the testimony of the police and the investigation they performed. He also knows that each officer is bestowed with an invisible "shroud of veracity" by virtue of the esteem with which police are generally held in the community.

People believe and want to believe that police officers are honest and lack deceit. The whole jury has anticipated, since the voir dire (jury selection) the moment the testifying officer is called by the bailiff as a witness. That officer is scrutinized the moment her foot hits the floor as she steps through the door and enters the courtroom. From head to foot. If the officer walks confidently, dressed professionally, and with personal pride in her appearance, the jury extends the courtesy of belief. That believability cannot be damaged by anything that the defense may have done or attempts to do, but it can be stripped away by incompetent, insincere, or dishonest testimony.

The penalty for false testimony for any other witness is to be labelled a perjurer and to be forgotten. The penalty for a police officer who is incompetent or dishonest is a verdict of acquittal for the defendant and a prosecutor who may not prosecute that officer's cases.

PREPARING FOR TRIAL

Habit is a tool or a vice. If from habit all investigations are conducted with the same meticulousness, a habit aimed at success has been established. That habit is difficult to cultivate because police know that the majority of investigations leading to arrest will never go to trial. If the case is not likely to be tried, why invest time and effort writing? Presuming cases will not go to trial or that another officer will do the writing assures embarrassment or dishonesty when that presumption fails. The only foolproof way to avoid falling victim to the "plea bargain" presumption is to prepare every case as though it were going to trial. It may be tedious, but it certainly provides practice. After all, practice makes a defense lawyer's life more difficult.

The easiest way for a prosecutor to obtain a plea bargain from a knowledgeable defense lawyer is to convince that lawyer that the case is ready to try and that the prosecutor is confident of the outcome. Much of the paperwork generated as part of the investigation is discoverable by the defense. If a competent defense lawyer discovers shoddy and inaccurate data included in the police investigation, why plead out?

An officer with experience testifying will not wait until the day of trial to review the case. It would be prudent to examine the paperwork, evidence, logs, photographs, diagrams, sketches, and charts that will be admitted through the officer's testimony. Review the condition of all evidence, including markings, labels, and chain of custody.

IDENTIFICATION

Before a witness may testify, it is necessary to describe who the witness is, what that individual can contribute to the case in question and why this person should be allowed to testify. In determining why the person should be allowed to testify, the court must determine the relevance and the scope of the prospective testimony. The predicate (foundation that allows police testimony) for a police officer would include the following type of questions:

1. Question: Will you state your name please.
   Answer: Respond with full legal name.
2. Question: What is your occupation.
   Answer: Give specific function and organization, e.g., police officer with the under water recovery team for the Austin Police Department.
3. Question: To be a police officer in Austin, Texas is it necessary to be certified?

	Answer:	A simple "yes."
4.	Question:	Are you certified?
	Answer:	A simple "yes."
5.	Question:	What is required by your department for an officer to become certified?
	Answer:	Relate the number of weeks at the academy, field training, and probationary period.
6.	Question:	What are your duties as a member of the underwater recovery team?
	Answer:	To respond to official requests for underwater search and recovery of evidence.
7.	Question:	Is there any special training or certification required for officers working on the underwater recovery team?
	Answer:	Provide a description of all dive training and certification required and obtained.
8.	Question:	What is required by your department for an officer to serve as a member of the underwater recovery team?
	Answer:	Discuss SCUBA certification requirements, advanced certification, specialized dive training, underwater archaeological education, and any departmental requirements.
9.	Question:	Were you working (date in question).
	Answer:	Yes.
10.	Question:	Were you dispatched to a particular location at approximately (hour of dispatch).
	Answer:	Yes.
11.	Question:	What was that location?
	Answer:	Describe area to which you and the team were dispatched, e.g., Town Lake, Austin, Texas. The specific location as to city and state are elements that the prosecutor must prove during the course of the prosecution.

The prosecutor must prove that the State has jurisdiction of the place in question and that the specific court is the appropriate place (venue) for the case to be tried. Failure to prove either of these two elements may result in a "directed verdict of acquittal" for the defendant. Police have little difficulty in understanding that specific offenses have elements but are often ignorant of the jurisdictional and venue elements required in every case. The investigating officer is the most probable source for soliciting this information. Be prepared for the question, it is not as innocuous as it sounds.

12.	Question:	Based on that call, what did you do?
	Answer:	Describe team gathering, equipment loading, briefing, and transport to search embarkation point.
13.	Question:	Upon arriving on the scene what actions, if any, did you take?
	Answer:	Describe the recovery operation, including, the search, discovery of evidence, photographing, measuring, tagging, marking, bagging, and transportation of any evidence.

Recovery team members can anticipate these types of questions and should be prepared to answer them. Ideally, the prosecutor and prospective police witnesses should meet to cover the testimony and the evidence.

A trial blueprint should be constructed as a result of that meeting containing an overview of the testimony necessary to "prove up" all evidence. Many prosecutors will expect that you already know what testimony is expected and will devote little time in pretrial discussions. The other possibility is that a new prosecutor may not be sure of what his responsibility is let alone try to prepare police for their testimonial load. It is an inexperienced prosecutor who will find a knowledgeable police witness invaluable. Making yourself invaluable is not a bad career perspective.

CHAIN OF CUSTODY

Under the common law, a chain of custody must be shown from the moment evidence was discovered until it appears in the courtroom, so that the court can be satisfied that what the prosecutor is attempting to have entered into evidence is the same thing that was discovered by the police and has not been altered. Evidence should be handled only by people with a need to handle it. That need should be predicated on something other than curiosity.

The officer who recovers a particular item of evidence will be responsible for testifying to what has happened to the evidence since it was recovered at the search site. Other than packaging, storing and testing, the best thing that can happen to evidence is nothing. Every time the evidence is removed from storage it should be recorded. If persons other than the testifying officer have handled the evidence, they may then be called by the defense to testify. They will be asked the purpose for removal, procedures of removal, where it was taken, what was done to it, and most importantly, if there is any way to be sure that the item labelled as a specific bit of evidence might not have been inadvertently substituted with another similar item. It avoids unnecessary testimony, confusion, and innuendo if the officer who is to "prove up" the evidence retrieves it and brings it to the courtroom.

Most evidence tags contain hearsay evidence, it is a mistake to anticipate that objection and remove evidence tags prior to trial. The evidence tags can be removed at the time of trial once they have been identified for the record. All prospective exhibits (evidence to be admitted into evidence) should be brought to the courthouse prior to the day's court activity so that the prosecutor can have the court reporter mark each piece of evidence with a chronological adhesive exhibit tag. Evidence should be checked with the evidence log compiled during the investigation to assure that all evidence has been retrieved. Chain of custody testimony is basically the same for all evidence. Chain of custody is not proven until the evidence has been appropriately identified. Authentication is a process separate from establishing the chain of custody and differs depending on the specific evidence to be entered. This authentication is often referred to as a "predicate" for admissibility. Specific predicates will be discussed later.

Officers often flounder around after being asked a question that should have been recognized as part of a chain of custody predicate. It is the responsibility of the testifying officers to sufficiently understand the rules of evidence to enable them to testify competently. In every situation in which evidence is to be admitted, the testifying officer should anticipate chain of custody inquiries. The chain of custody is proven by a series of questions containing the following or similar queries:

1. Question: I will show you what has been marked as State's Exhibit Number 1, and ask you if you have seen it before?

   Answer: Do not at this juncture identify what is being proffered; simply answer, "yes."

2. Question: Can you describe it?

   Answer: This is a request for a brief generic description not a detailed description, a more detailed characterization will be solicited once the chain of custody has been established.

3. Question: When and where did you first see it?

   Answer: A specific date, time and location will answer this question satisfactorily.

4. Question: What did you do with State's Exhibit Number 1 when you saw it?

   Answer: This question can be answered by describing how the item was marked, bagged, and tagged.

5. Question: How do you know that State's Exhibit Number 1 is the same (generic description of evidence such as, firearm, shirt, etc.) that you recovered?

   Answer: This question is designed to allow the testifying officer to testify to the marks placed on the evidence by the investigator or to the signed tape used to seal containers in which evidence not susceptible to marking have been placed.

6. Question: Other than the addition of the Identifying mark and State's Exhibit sticker, has it been altered in any way?

   Answer: Obviously, if the evidence has been subjected to testing, it has probably been altered. The nature of the alteration should be explained including how the item was transported to the testing facilities and returned from those facilities. The evidence tag and ledger should contain all testing information including: time out, destination, purpose, handlers, time in, and a description of how it was stored while out of the evidence room. Much of that information will be testified to by the persons receiving and testing the evidence. It may take a number of witnesses to prove an adequate chain of custody.

7. Question: Is it in the same or similar condition as when you first saw it?
   Answer: The answer to this question is a simple "yes," however, testing may severely alter the item. If it has been altered, the appropriate answer is to describe the alterations and then attest that it is in substantially the same or similar condition but for those alterations.
8. Question: How did State's Exhibit Number 1 get to the courtroom today.
   Answer: The best answer is for the testifying officer to have transported it.

The defendant has the opportunity to cross-examine the witness who is attempting to establish the chain of custody. This inquiry, done before the prosecutor has passed the witness, is referred to as voir dire of the witness. The jury selection process is also called voir dire. The reason both processes are called voir dire is in the literal translation of the French, meaning to "speak the truth." The request to voir dire can be made at two junctures during the prosecution's direct examination of a witness: during chain of custody determination and when qualifying an expert witness. The request by the defense is simply an attempt to develop testimony that will allow the defense to challenge the chain of custody or the qualifications of the expert.

AUTHENTICATION

Once the witness has been identified and the chain of custody has been established, the evidence will require authentication before the court will admit the exhibit into evidence. Chain of custody testimony evolved to assure that an item attempting to be admitted into evidence has not been altered, while in police custody. Authentication evolved to assist in establishing that items, not self-authenticating, sought to be admitted into evidence are what the lawyer claims them to be. A self-authenticating item is one that requires no assistance in establishing its authenticity. A certified copy of a birth certificate requires no elaborate protocol to establish that it is in fact a certified birth certificate. Self-authenticating items are usually set out in State and Federal Rules of Evidence. If the item is not self-authenticating then an "Admissibility Predicate" must be laid.

Various types of exhibits must be authenticated by someone with knowledge of how the item came into the possession of the police and what it is. Generally the same person establishing chain of custody will authenticate the exhibit.

Photographs

1. Question: Do you recognize the contents of the photograph that you have identified as State's Exhibit Number 1?
   Answer: Yes.
2. Question: Does the photograph fairly and accurately represent the scene as you recall it?
   Answer: Yes.

At this point the prosecutor would offer the exhibit into evidence. An evidence offer usually begins by the prosecutor tendering the exhibit to the defense for any objections. If the defense objects, and the likelihood of objections increases directly in proportion to the importance of the exhibit to the prosecution's case, the defense may choose to voir dire the witness on the authenticity of the exhibit. If the judge sustains any defense objections, it may be necessary for the prosecutor to attempt to address those objections by laying a further predicate. Having listened to the objection and the discussion pertaining to that objection, the testifying officer should have a good idea of what additional predicate need be laid. Once the matter of the defense objections has been satisfactorily resolved the exhibit will be accepted by the judge as evidence. The prosecutor may now ask questions that will allow a description of the contents of the photograph and the significance of those contents.

Diagrams, Maps, Plats

1. Question: Did you participate in the preparation of the diagram that you have identified as State's Exhibit Number 2?
   Answer: Yes.
2. Question: Are you personally familiar with the objects and locations contained in the diagram?
   Answer: Yes.
3. Question: Is this a fair and accurate representation of the _____ (search site, recovery site, location of evidence found) as you recall it?
   Answer: Yes.
4. Question: Is this diagram drawn to scale?
   Answer: No.

Generally, it is easier to testify about a diagram that is not drawn to scale. Defense lawyers may focus on miniscule measurement errors to undermine the credibility of the entire diagram. If all underwater measurements are linked to a permanent landmark that was located on the diagram with the aid of surveying instruments, having a scale drawing may not be a problem. Reasonable approximations are much easier to defend.

Considerable time will be taken to explain the map and plats of an underwater operation once they have been authenticated. Original notes from which the measurements were taken may prove helpful during trial. Everything that was noted during the underwater operation may not have been included on the site map. If the defense begins asking technical questions pertaining to measurement procedures the field notes may assist in refreshing recollection.

A caveat must be offered whenever field notes are retained and used on the witness stand. If field notes are used on the witness stand to refresh memory or as a resource, those notes must be made available to the defense upon request. Anything written in or on the notes will be relinquished. The witness does not have the right to remove anything from the notes to which she has referred, they must be turned over immediately to the defense for examination.

Occasionally, embarrassing material is contained in a field notebook. This is material that may not be relevant to the trial. If it is in the notebook it is discoverable by the defendant. Although irrelevant, if it can be used to discredit the witness it will be allowed.

Another rule allows the defense access to any written materials that the witness has used to prepare for court. Anticipate this question and be ready to produce any material that was instrumental in trial preparation.

Video Recordings

Today's investigator relies on photography to record the crime scene. Underwater crime scenes lend themselves, visibility permitting, to video recording as well as still photography. The predicate for video recordings is often confused with the predicate for audio recordings. The appropriate predicate combines the audio recording and still photograph predicate.

1. Question: Was the videotape you have described as State's Exhibit Number 3 prepared on a recording device capable of making an accurate recording?
   Answer: Yes.

No technical data need be supplied; however, if the witness is a competent video technician, a brief technical description may ensue. However, technical understanding is not required to use videotape equipment nor to establish the predicate for admissibility.

2. Question: Who was the operator?
   Answer: I was (or insert name of party making video).

It is not necessary to have actually filmed the video to be able to prove it up. All that is required is that the testifying officer has viewed the scene prior to filming, has viewed the film and the film is an accurate reflection of the scene.

3. Question: Have you viewed the tape?
   Answer: Yes.
4. Question: Has the videotape been altered in any way?
   Answer: No.

Some agencies will voice-over a tape to provide a more understanding viewing of the video images. Obviously, the voice-over is hearsay and probably inadmissible. If the defense objects to the voice-over, the volume can simply be turned off. It may be necessary to testify that the video has been altered by the addition of a sound track but that the addition has not altered the video images.

5. Question: When was the tape made?
   Answer: Provide time and date.
6. Question: Do the pictures of the events contained in the videotape fairly and accurately reflect the scene as you recall it.
   Answer: Yes.

PHYSICAL EVIDENCE

Every investigation involves physical evidence and every investigation should anticipate the need for authenticating each item discovered. Authentication of physical evidence is fairly standard and should pose no admissibility problems for the testifying officer. Occasionally, defense lawyers will stipulate to the authenticity of large quantities of evidence when they are convinced that the testifying witness is competent in establishing the appropriate predicate. This stipulation avoids the dramatic effect of the prosecution focusing on each piece of evidence.

1. Question: You have in your hand a _____ (handgun, knife, bat, hatchet, shirt, gasoline can, etc.) that you have identified as State's Exhibit 4. When and where did you first see it?
   Answer: Time, date, and location.
2. Question: How do you know that it is the same _____ (handgun, knife, bat, hatchet, shirt, gasoline can, etc.) that you recovered?
   Answer: Describe identifying characteristics. If there are no specific identifying characteristics that distinguish this item from all others, then it should be marked and that mark described.
3. Question: Is the _____ in the same or substantially the same condition as when you found it?
   Answer: Describe any alterations.

MULTIPLE PREDICATES

Often it will take more than one witness to lay the complete predicate for a piece of evidence. For example, a recovery team diver recovers a handgun and after proper measuring and handling gives it to an evidence technician to check for latent prints on the ammunition contained in the magazine. The evidence technician discovers latent prints and manages to successfully lift one. A suspect has inked fingerprint impressions taken. The latent print and the inked impression are forwarded to the crime laboratory for comparison. It will take the testimony of four witnesses before the laboratory analysis can be admitted as evidence;

1. The diver who discovered the handgun will identify the weapon and attest to the fact that it is the one found, describe the method employed in discovery, and testify that it has not been altered.

2. The technician who lifted the latent print will extend the custody chain, identify the weapon, identify the latent, describe the method whereby a latent can be lifted, and attest that it has not been altered.

3. The officer taking the inked impression of the suspect will identify the inked impression, identify the defendant from whom the impression was taken, and attest that it has not been altered.

4. The laboratory technician will extend the custody chain for both the inked and latent prints, identify both, and express an opinion regarding the laboratory comparison that was made.

As each witness testifies, the prosecutor will request that provisional admissibility be allowed the exhibit pending the anticipated cumulative testimony of all four witnesses. After all four witnesses have testified, the prosecutor should have overcome any objections as to the authenticity of the exhibit offered, and the court should allow the exhibit into evidence.

EXPERT WITNESSES

One cannot testify as an expert witness unless it can be demonstrated, to the satisfaction of the court, that the prospective expert has some special skill or knowledge that will assist the trier of fact (judge or jury) in understanding the facts in issue. It is therefore incumbent upon the judge to determine whether the prospective expert has such specialized knowledge which will in fact assist in furthering his or the jury's understanding of any issues in question. It is the purpose of a qualifying hearing to allow the adversaries to establish the credentials of and need for a prospective expert. This hearing takes place during the normal course of trial and is virtually indistinguishable to the lay person. It appears to be a direct examination of a witness with an emphasis on background and specialization. Since the hearing takes place during the course of the trial, it is seldom viewed as a hearing but rather part of the normal trial process. The scope of the hearing is restricted to the qualifications of the witness and the need for the expert's assistance. Often the credentials of the expert will go unchallenged by the opposition and the direct examination begins without hesitation. However, should there be some question as to the competence of the expert or the need for such testimony, the opposition will interrupt the "expert offer" after qualifying questions have been asked, and request the court allow the witness to be voir dired as to competence and necessity. In many courts, after qualifying questions have been asked and answered, the party calling the witness will make a request of the court that the witness be accepted as an expert witness; this is referred to as offering the witness. It is good practice to make an "expert offer" in that it tells the jury something special has just happened and it conveys to the opposition that the offer of proof pertaining to the witness' expertise is complete and the time for requesting an opportunity to voir dire the expert has arrived.

Underwater investigators are a relatively new phenomenon and qualifying such an expert poses some unique questions. It is impossible today to obtain formal education in underwater criminalistics, so one cannot use college credentials in a direct fashion. Experience, training, and education will be the road to qualification for the underwater expert. College courses in archaeology, marine archaeology, criminalistics, or forensics will serve as a substantial foundation for scientific testimony. Scuba certification, advanced dive training, dive experience, and training in criminal investigation should complete the underwater expert qualification predicate. Often, police divers identify themselves on the witness stand as certified divers and give testimony about the recovery of certain items of evidence. As underwater criminalists, courts will grow to expect a lengthy litany of education, training, and service for expert qualification, because as the field grows, so will the competence and credentials of those providing such services.

Scientific Evidence

Scientific evidence can come before the jury only from the mouth of an expert witness. Occasionally, controversy surrounds a particular scientific or pseudoscientific practice bringing into question whether such a practice or procedure is in fact scientific. The United States Court of Appeals set forth a rule that has been followed for years, known as the Frye test. The Frye test simply postulated that scientific evidence could not be admitted until it had gained general acceptance in the particular field to which it belonged (*Frye v. United States,* 293 F. 1013, 1923). It is this test that has been used in determining the scientific validity of hypnosis, polygraphs, battered women's syndrome, DNA printing, and others. Many courts have paid little attention to the Frye standard and employed individual judicial discretion in the determination of what is scientific and what is not. The United States Supreme Court has decided that Federal Rule of Evidence 702 supersedes the Frye test (*Daubert v. Merrell-Dow Pharmaceuticals, Inc.,* 113 S. Ct. 2793, 1993). Rule 702 deals with the admissibility of expert testimony and provides that "if scientific, technical, or other specialized knowledge will assist the trier of fact to understand the evidence or to determine a fact in issue, a witness qualified as an expert by knowledge, skill, experience, training or education may testify thereto in the form of an opinion or otherwise." If Frye is no longer the standard, then what standard is to apply. That Frye was replaced by the Federal Rules of Evidence does not imply that there are no restrictions on scientific testimony. Under the rules the trial judge must ensure that any and all scientific testimony or evidence admitted is not only relevant, but reliable (*Daubert v. Merrell-Dow Pharmaceuticals, Inc.,* 113 S.Ct. 2795, 1993). The trial judge must consider whether the technique employed is replicable, has been subjected to peer review and publication and to what extent has the technique been accepted by the scientific community.

The standards set forth by McCormick in his law journal article entitled "Scientific Evidence: Defining a New Approach to Admissibility" would provide greater guidance in determining the probative value of proffered scientific evidence. McCormack offers eleven factors to be applied in a probative analysis of scientific evidence offers:

1. The potential error rate in using the technique;
2. The existence and maintenance of standards governing its use;
3. Presence of safeguards in the characteristics of the technique;
4. Analogy to other scientific techniques whose results are admissible;

5. The extent to which the technique has been accepted by scientists in the field involved;
6. The nature and breadth of the inference adduced;
7. The clarity and simplicity with which the technique can be described and its results explained;
8. The extent to which the basic data are verifiable by the court and jury;
9. The availability of other experts to test and evaluate the technique;
10. The probative significance of the evidence in the circumstances of the case;
11. The care with which the technique was employed in the case (McCormack, 1982).

The simplest test to apply to any suggested scientific procedure is the replicability of the procedure and the opportunity to test the validity of test results. Applying such standards will reduce the arbitrary discretion of trial courts in admitting astrological and junk food influences on defendants.

Fingerprints

Although fingerprints are often the basis for the solution to movie homicides, fingerprints are more often effective in eliminating individuals from the list of possible suspects. The predicate for fingerprint evidence has been around for a long time and most investigators know it by heart. The primary objection to fingerprint testimony invariably revolves around the number of classifiable ridge characteristics.

1. Question: What are your duties with the Austin Police Department?
   Answer: Underwater Recovery Team evidence technician.
2. Question: As an evidence technician have you been called upon to identify and lift fingerprints?
   Answer: Yes.
3. Question: What training and background do you have that qualifies you as a fingerprint identification expert?
   Answer: Describe all relevant education, training, and experience.
4. Question: How long have you been employed as an evidence technician?
   Answer: Provide the length of employment as a fingerprint technician or investigator.
5. Question: Have you testified in court before pertaining to fingerprint identification?
   Answer: Yes.
6. Question: On how many prior occasions?

	Answer:	An approximation will do unless a specific record has been maintained to corroborate each instance.
7.	Question:	What is a fingerprint?
	Answer:	The pattern of friction skin ridges found on the palm side of the finger and thumbs. Whatever the answer, keep it in language lay people can understand. If a word of art is used, take time to explain it to the jury.
8.	Question:	What is a latent print?
	Answer:	When a finger touches a surface perspiration and oil is transferred onto the touched surface leaving an impression of the finger's ridge pattern.
9.	Question:	What is an inked impression?
	Answer:	For the purposes of comparison a finger can be covered with ink and pressed against a piece of paper leaving the finger ridge pattern.
10.	Question:	Is it possible to retrieve a latent print from an object that has been submerged and match it with a known inked impression?
	Answer:	Yes.
11.	Question:	I will hand you State's Exhibit Number 5 and ask you if you recognize it?
	Answer:	Yes.
12.	Question:	What is it?
	Answer:	It is a fingerprint that was lifted from a bullet that had been loaded into the magazine of a submerged handgun.

The handgun, bullet, and print would most likely have been entered into evidence by the diver who discovered the weapon and the technician who had lifted the latent.

13.	Question:	How do you recognize it?
	Answer:	Evidence recovered from underwater locations will be examined, once recovered, for latent prints. Lifted prints will have been photographed, sealed in plastic and labelled or sealed intact on the object upon which the impression was left. Identifying the label's contents will identify the print.

Comparisons can be made from a photograph if the latent was destroyed in the attempt to lift it. That is why it is important to photograph the latent image before trying to lift it.

14.	Question:	Where and when did you first see it?
	Answer:	Time, date, and location of first underwater viewing.
15.	Question:	I will now hand you State's Exhibit Number 6 and ask you if you recognize it?
	Answer:	Yes.
16.	Question:	What is it?
	Answer:	An inked fingerprint card.
17.	Question:	Who made it?
	Answer:	State the name of the officer who inked the impressions on the fingerprint card. If the testifying expert inked the impressions then questions 18, 19, 20 and 21 would be asked.
18.	Question:	When did you make it?
	Answer:	Approximate time and date.
19.	Question:	Where did you make it?
	Answer:	Location.

20. Question: Is the person from whom these inked fingerprint impressions were taken present in the courtroom today?
    Answer: Yes.
21. Question: Would you point him out please?
    Answer: The witness will generally point her finger and the prosecutor will say "let the record reflect that the witness has identified the defendant." The record will only reflect what has been said. The narrative by the prosecutor is not testimony. Using the "record reflecting" approach may result in a questionable in-court identification of the defendant. The appropriate response is to describe the defendant and his location, e.g., he is the gentleman with the blue sport coat sitting at the defense counsel table next to the defense attorney. Now the in-court identification of the defendant will withstand appellate scrutiny.
22. Question: Did you perform a comparison of the prints on State's Exhibit Number 5 with the prints on State's Exhibit Number 6?
    Answer: Yes.
23. Question: Based upon that comparison, do you have an opinion as to whether or not the finger prints marked as State's Exhibit Number 5 belong to the defendant?
    Answer: Yes. Do not yet express that opinion.
24. Question: What is that opinion?
    Answer: The prints on State's Exhibit 5 belong to the defendant.

Cross-examination by the defense will probably go into the method of comparison and the number of matching ridge characteristics. The expert should have a blow-up of the latent impressions mounted side by side on a chart so that in-court comparison can be made. Enlarged comparative prints are very effective in overwhelming the jury with the number of matching ridge characteristics.

The question always arises as to how many ridge characteristic comparisons are necessary for a positive identification. Experts vary as to the number required, usually somewhere between 10 and 20. There are over 150 individual ridge patterns on a full print. Most latents are partial prints, thereby raising the question of how many is enough. No statistical study to date has been done upon which a definitive number has been obtained. It is therefore up to the individual expert, based on knowledge and experience, to determine whether there are sufficient ridge characteristics to warrant an opinion as to the comparative value of a latent print. The fewer matching ridge patterns, the higher the probability the defense will present its own fingerprint expert to rebut the State's expert. The greater number of matching ridge characteristics the less likely a lengthy cross examination.

Trace Evidence

1. Question: What are your duties?
   Answer: Laboratory technician, forensic scientist, etc.
2. Question: What educational background do you have that qualifies you for your duties?
   Answer: Describe in detail experience, education, and training.
3. Question: Have you received any specialized training in the area of _____ (hair, fiber, etc.) analysis and comparison?
   Answer: Describe all workshops, seminars, college courses, etc.
4. Question: Have you taught any courses in _____ (hair, fiber, etc.) analysis and comparison?
   Answer: This question will only be asked if applicable. It would not impress the judge or jury to have to answer such a question "no."
5. Question: Have you written any articles?
   Answer: If applicable list all publications.

The idea is to frustrate the opposition with the quality of the credentials of the expert to the point the opposition is willing to stipulate that the witness is an acceptable expert. Such a stipulation, however, is seldom accepted. Lawyers want all the credentials of their experts before the court, after all those credentials are part of what the expert is being paid for. In the battle of experts the game is to hire an expert who looks better than the opposition's.

6. Question: Have you testified as an expert before?
   Answer: Yes or no.
7. Question: How many times.
   Answer: A reasonable approximation will do.

In most instances an expert who works for the State is expected to have considerable trial experience. Experts who do not work for the state, such as psychologists or psychiatrists, are scrutinized as to their trial experience. These individuals should be objective and that objectivity can be undermined if the majority of courtroom testimony has been prosecutorial.

8. Question: How is a _____ (hair, fiber, etc.) analysis performed?
   Answer: A sample of the trace material and the material to be compared are placed under the lens of a comparison microscope to determine the extent of the association between the trace material recovered and the comparison sample.
9. Question: I will hand you what has been marked as State's Exhibit Number 7 and ask you if you recognize it?
   Answer: Yes.
10. Question: What is it?
    Answer: A _____ (hair, fiber, etc.) sample provided me by investigators taken from the crime scene.

11. Question: When and where did you first see it?
    Answer: Date and location.
12. Question: How do you recognize it?
    Answer: By the label on the container.
13. Question: Let me now hand you State's Exhibit Number 8 and ask you if you recognize it?
    Answer: Yes.
14. Question: What is it?
    Answer: A _____ (hair, fiber, etc.) taken from the defendant (or from the defendant's home, auto, or clothing).
15. Question: When and where did you first see it?
    Answer: Date and location.
16. Question: Were you asked to conduct a comparison of State's Exhibit 7 and State's Exhibit 8?
    Answer: Yes.
17. Question: Did you perform such a comparison?
    Answer: Yes.
18. Question: How did you conduct the comparison?
    Answer: This question should be answered with specificity but in language the jury can understand.
19. Question: Did these two exhibits have any characteristics in common?
    Answer: Yes.
20. Question: What characteristics did these two exhibits have in common?
    Answer: Explain the matching characteristics of the two specimens using an enlargement of the photomicrograph image.
21. Question: Based on your comparison of these two exhibits, have you formed an opinion about them?
    Answer: Yes.
22. Question: What is that opinion?
    Answer: Opinions pertaining to trace material comparison are usually expressed in terms of "more likely than not" as opposed to the type of unequivocal opinion of fingerprint comparison.

Most scientific experts providing testimony pursuant to a police investigation will be required to assist in laying a predicate for their opinions based on evidence provided by investigators who generally do not have a science background. By understanding the predicate required for the admission of test results and expert opinions, investigators will be less likely to contaminate or mishandle evidence. Investigators will also be able to provide specific information that expert witnesses will be able to rely upon in their tests and opinions. This chapter was not included to make investigators and dive recovery team members forensic experts but to provide the context within which recovered evidence is used.

REFERENCES

Anderson, K. and Bradley, J. 1992. *Texas Predicate Manual.* Austin: Texas District and County Attorneys Association.

Saltzburg and Redden. 1986. *Federal Rules of Evidence Manual,* 4th ed.

McCormick, Scientific evidence: Defining a new approach to admissibility, *67 Iowa L. Rev. 879:*911–912, 1982.

TABLE OF CASES

Daubert v Merrell-Dow Pharmaceuticals, Inc., 113 S Ct. 2786, 1993.

Frye v. United States, 293 F. 1013 (D.C Cir. 1923).

Chapter 11

THE FUTURE

It is not difficult to forecast what the future holds for underwater criminalists. As in every other aspect of the criminal justice system it will be but a short time before underwater recovery teams are overwhelmed with a workload that will require that only the most serious of offenses be accorded the "full treatment." As underwater recovery becomes more scientific, greater educational and training demands will be placed on those seeking to work as a dive team member. Presently that training is a product of "on-the-job" exposure. In time, agencies will provide specialized training opportunities for those departments that wish to increase the competence of their dive operations. Budgets will be expanded to provide for training and equipment, if not voluntarily, then as a product of cost benefit analysis or lawsuits arising from injuries resulting from equipment or training inadequacies.

Much of the technology that has evolved in marine archaeology was a product of necessity and imagination. Police divers will discover needs unique to the underwater processing of secondary crime scenes and accident scenes. Those needs will give rise to innovation in technique and equipment. The underwater investigator of today is the pioneer who will lay the foundation for future operations and the tools that will be used. Crime scenes that heretofore went undetected or unsolved will be viewed through a different looking glass. Procedures employed in the past will be replaced by methodology and organization. As diving equipment becomes safer and easier to use, more emphasis will be placed on recruiting those with analytical abilities and less emphasis on physical prowess.

The diving business is one of risk and equipment should be such as to minimize risk. However, the evolution of the underwater criminalist must not become preoccupied with budget, equipment, and sophisticated hardware. The basic tools of the investigator and criminalist above or below the water are the ability to recognize and preserve physical evidence.

The crime scene (primary or secondary) and the accident scene are the first step in the process of using scientific inquiry in an investigation. All the resources of the investigator, criminalist, or crime laboratory will be rendered useless if evidence is left undiscovered, ignored, or contaminated.

If underwater recovery teams are to make an impact in underwater investigative outcomes, it is necessary to transcend the mere appointment of police personnel who will provide a dive recovery function and be included in the agency's table of organization. Appointments cannot be made on considerations other than fitness and prospective contribution. The effective recovery team will not be measured by the hardware, machinery, and mobile units it can field, but rather, by the quality of services they perform. The underwater recovery dive team must be recognized as the essential first step in underwater crime scene processing and as an integral part of the total investigative and forensic service offered by the agency.

The careful selection, education, and training of prospective team members is critical in establishing and maintaining the quality of the underwater recovery specialist. Police administrators have a responsibility to select the personnel to perform investigations. They cannot abrogate the responsibility to create and foster training programs that will assure competent and safe investigative performance.

Although continued in-service training is essential to insure the safe and successful operation of a dive team, many agencies will claim that lack of time, space, desire, or money prevents them from making a commitment to continuous upgrading of specialized skills. It is therefore incumbent upon universities and colleges to provide the educational support that agencies cannot or will not provide. Field Archaeology and Marine Archaeology should become recommended electives for students pursuing degrees in criminal justice or law enforcement who may be interested in the processing of underwater crime scenes. Scuba certification should be encouraged as part of physical education electives. Introductory criminalistics or forensics courses should be adopted by institutions offering degrees in law enforcement. Universities and colleges are not responsible for training police officers but they do have an obligation to supplement scientific skills for the university student seeking investigative specialization. Just as marine archaeology became a legitimate educational pursuit independent of field archaeology, so must underwater criminalistics become an area of study independent of criminal investigation or forensics. Science is and must be an integral part of law enforcement and must become an integral part of the criminal justice curriculum.

Universities must recognize the need for adopting graduate and undergraduate degrees in the forensic sciences as absolutely essential to meet the increasing manpower needs law enforcement has and will continue to place on the profession. Few colleges and universities offer courses or degrees in forensics, criminalistics or marine archaeology. Such skills are recruited out of the ranks of college graduates who have received their education in the sciences. Although schooled in scientific method, analysis, and inquiry, few have any real understanding of the skills utilized in the processing of the underwater crime scene. Not only must the new underwater criminalist learn to apply specialized skills in the excavation and recordation of the underwater crime scene, she must also develop more than a passing familiarity with forensics and the operation of the crime laboratory.

In addition to the technical skills of the underwater forensic investigator, the new team member must master the skills of an expert witness. An ability to keep accurate records and to communicate the content of those records is necessary to properly and effectively present the investigation in a context and a language that a judge and a jury understand and appreciate.

Obviously, education alone does not make a competent investigator above or below the water. However, many police agencies are requiring candidates to have some college and others provide incentives for obtaining college credit while employed. The future will bring the day when police work becomes a profession, when police are paid a salary commensurate with their responsibilities and risks taken. Society must recognize that a community gets the quality of law enforcement that it pays for.

Education, experience, perception, persistence, and judgment are all essential characteristics of the investigator and the criminalist. When combined with careful screening and selection of qualified personnel the final product should be a competent underwater forensic investigator equipped to pave the road to the future.

As more investigators become versed in the methods employed by marine archaeologists, the quality of underwater investigations will increase. With the improvement in quality of underwater recovery operations will come an improvement in the quality of the testimony based upon the documentation reflecting the recovery operation. As it becomes apparent that underwater recovery teams are more than salvage operators, agencies and officers within those agencies will begin viewing underwater operations with new respect and acceptance. Once police have established the viability of applying marine archaeological methods to underwater processing of evidence, once courts and prosecutors accept no less, underwater investigation will become as common as any other aspect of criminal investigation.

Those departments with police dive teams will be the first to employ the methods described in this book. As those methods produce results, agencies without dive recovery teams will request assistance from nearby agencies that have underwater recovery capabilities and hasten acceptance of the underwater criminal archaeologist. The first major air disaster wherein methods described in this book are applied may receive sufficient media attention to provide the necessary exposure to garner widespread public awareness and acceptance of this new approach to underwater criminal investigation.

INDEX